Contemplations

Herbert Windolf

ISBN: 1979106312
ISBN 13: 9781979106313

Publications by Herbert Windolf,
As Translator of Karl May

Published by Washington State University Press:
The Oil Prince

Published through BookSurge:
Black Mustang
with Marlies Bugman

Published by Nemsi Books:
The Treasure of Silver Lake
The Ghost of Llano Estacado
The Son of the Bear Hunter
Imaginary Journeys I
Imaginary Journeys II
Imaginary Journeys III
Thoughts of Heaven
Winnetou IV
Pacific Shores
The Inca's Legacy
The Scout
Deadly Dust
The Mahdi I

Published through CreateSpace:
The Mahdi II
The Mahdi III
One more Day . . .
As Translator of Autobiography of Isabell Steiner

As Author of Poetic Prose:
Observations and Reflections
Pondering What Is
Otherwise
Musings

Private Printing:
Biography – Bridges across Times and Continents

Published by Verlag für Tiefenpsychologie und Anthropologie:
Brücken über Zeiten und Kontinente
Biography – with Dorothea Rutkowsky

Table of Contents

Introduction

Writing and re-reading my poems, written through the years, I feel a great kinship with the French essayist, Michel de Montaigne, the inventor of the essay, or *essai* in French, who lived four hundred years ago.

Candidly and honestly he wrote in short tracts about his observations, his thoughts – and much more sophisticated than I do – the daily events of his life, and the culture and problems of his time.

My own poetic prose is more brief and comes in a somewhat lyrical form, but I feel it is similar to the great man's writings.

This, my fifth volume of what I have named poetic prose in my fourth, is a compendium of my world laid down in close to one thousand poems. The titles of my publications reflect my concerns and thought processes. At times I have managed to slip in a funny one.

My first has been *Observations and Reflections*, the second, *Pondering What Is*, the third, *Otherwise*, and the forth, *Musings*. Number five, *Contemplations*, may be the last of my volumes. All of them are self-published.

Ideas for titles have shrunk a bit. Not that there isn't still plenty to write about Life. Have I grown tired? Not really. Maybe there's too much to say, and too much of it being of a negative nature representative of our time – as if previous times have not had their plethoras of troubles, if we go by Steven Pinker's research in his book *The Better Angels of our Nature*.

There is *a time for all seasons* and thus a time for my writings to end eventually.

But . . . as I have sometimes maintained in the past: I can change my mind and now, at eighty-one years of age, I take the liberty of not giving a hoot what others may think.

As always, however, I am immensely grateful to Lynn Chesson and Zene Krogh for editing and proof-reading my writings.

Cheers.

Herbert Windolf
Prescott, Arizona

Contemplations

Sometimes I am, sometimes I'm not.
At times I'm lost, then deep in thought.
There are times when I brood,
those aren't so good.
Then, here and there,
thoughts leap in the air like a frisky spring hare.
I like to explore what can and can't be,
what is and is not,
what's to be found towards windward and lee.
What the future may bring,
in the time I have left to explore and to see.

The passions are the only orators
that always persuade.
François de La Rochefoucauld

Encore

When love is lost,
can it rise once more,
from ashes abundant
to a triumphant encore?

For one human being to love another:
that is perhaps the most difficult of our tasks;
the ultimate, the last test and proof,
the work for which all other work is but preparation.
Rainer Maria Rilke

Change

The accelerating change of our time
is an existential threat
to the conservative mind,
whether individual or the communal kind.
Conservative parties, religions, too,
especially structured Islam,
are sorely tried by social, economic,
commercial, scientific, and technological change,
and threatened, lose their internal glue.
Some of the upsets we experience today
are the struggles of conservative minds
to maintain their accustomed way.
Yet, if they cannot stop change
their outlook is bleak,
and if they could stop it, return, rearrange,
the result might be worse,
as shown by the Syrian ISIS, so deranged.

Man is a rational animal who always loses his temper
when he is called upon to act in accordance
with the dictates of reason.
Oscar Wilde

Meaning

The world we know simply moves along.
Even stars and galaxies come and go.
Mountains rise, are eroded down.
Trees grow, then collapse and decompose.
Animals, before dying, feed, procreate,
once being born.
But that's not enough for the human spawn.
We want purpose between our dusk and dawn.
We create our meanings, right and wrong,
pursue them successful or failing
before our, oh so soon, swan song.
Ephemeral we are, most don't give it a thought,
until later in life, when it is too late.
It is all in vain, oh, how vain we are,
to think it matters what we contrive.
Nothing will outlive our lives.
The universe has no purpose,
and we are part of it.
It has no discernible meaning,
it simply is.

Order and simplification are the first steps
towards the mastery of a subject.
Thomas Mann

Creation 1

Imagine that one hundred thousand years ago
Man's world consisted only of concrete things
he could touch and see,
like rocks and food, the sun and the moon,
and if he lived there,
the surf, the crabs, and the vast open sea.
Then came the time when he imagined things,
created images in his mind,
like what pushed the sun and also the moon
day after day across the sky.
Having no understanding of its cause,
born from his mind was a spirit, a ghost.
Whichever way this came to be,
eventually inanimate, concrete ideas
in his mind became spiritual entities.
Evermore he created a world,
imaginary, fictitious, constructs of mind.
Myths were born, religions of all kinds,
so that today, the world we occupy consists,
for the most part, of constructs of mind.
As long as we agree on the one or the other,
they stay alive enabling us to work together.
But our fictions of mind arise, come and go.

When they've outlived their utility,
they are replaced by something new.
Give it a thought, hard as it may be,
eventually you may find that little is real.

I don't necessarily agree with everything I say.
Marshall McLuhan

Past, Present, and Future

I look at the land before my eyes
and here and there I try imagining at times
what it looked like a few hundred thousand,
some million years ago,
when volcanoes dotted Arizona,
when smoke, fire, ashes, and lava erupted, flowed,
and the land by giant creatures was toed.
At present the land looks so peaceful and calm,
houses dotting the forested hills,
a view to the soul of comfort and balm.
Then, when I imagine what lies ahead,
I fail, of course, for now I tread
on what cannot be known.
Maybe, when time's been long enough,
the Bradshaws will have been largely worn down.
But what of Man and his proud creations,
and what kind of creatures will roam these locations?

Life is not lost by dying; life is lost minute by minute,
day by dragging day, in all the thousand small uncaring ways.
Stephen Vincent Benét

Creation 2

Potential gave Man his immense success,
to cover the planet to its farthest recess.
At first he dealt only with concrete things,
like rocks and food, the rain, a mate,
but not of things that do not exist.
But he wondered why the sun crossed the sky,
and why, oh why, did his mate have to die?
It was the 'whys' that led him on
to give meaning to the unexplainable,
to create in his mind a world of his own.
Gnomes, and ghosts, and gods tumbled forth,
religions, corporations, and nations arose,
all constructs of his fertile mind.
What else will we create?
Whereto are we headed, humankind?

Disorder increases with time because we measure time
in the direction in which disorder increases.
Stephen Hawking

Literal

Some folks are literal,
take everything said exactly as true.
Others are much less so,
and use expressions, language,
as a playful avenue.
To tease, to allude, to insinuate, having fun,
and more often than not
for a good-natured pun.

Those who know their minds
do not necessarily know their hearts.
François de La Rochefoucauld

Tic-toc

Thus time went by.
Sitting in the stillness of night,
waiting for the siren's final cry,
that told of needing to seek shelter,
or, relieved, go to bed again, sleepy-eyed.
Thus, still today,
in the quiet of night,
when I hear this sound,
it tells me how and why
time goes by.
Tic-toc.

There is no greater pain than to remember,
in our present grief,
past happiness.
Dante Alighieri

People

For many years I've been interested in people,
their backgrounds, their outlooks, their desires, their lives.
Some of my own, I've shared many a time,
to establish trust, to say, "look, this is mine."
Sometimes to overcome the reluctance to talk,
when someone not used to it needed a spark.
Most others were happy being asked,
to talk of themselves, their present and past.
I've learned, found friendship,
at times just in passing, with others many decades to last.
Every life is a wonder – at least so, most,
and thus is of value,
this isn't a boast.

Two things I cannot understand: myself and others.
Erkki J. Jyrkkanen

Mantra,

words repeated to aid meditation,
most famous the Tibetan: Om Mani Padme Hum.
Half a year past I took a friend to the ER,
a blood clot in a leg needed taking him there.
Pumped full of medication the pain wouldn't fade,
so the nurse told him to sleep or to meditate.
As the scientist he was, meditation was strange.
He didn't know what to make of it,
for the pain to abate.
Thus, I said: "You need a mantra to concentrate,
to leave the world and pain behind."
To get him going, I said with a smirk:
keep repeating and repeating:
"Herb is a jerk."
He cracked up and laughed,
and at least for a minute,
the pain wasn't noticed.
The silly mantra had done its work.

Nature has placed mankind under the government
of two sovereign masters: pain and pleasure.
Jeremy Bentham

Chimera,

something wished for, illusory,
impossible to achieve,
but also a beast of Greek mythology
with a lion's head, a goat's body, a serpent's tail,
fire breathing, full of mischief.
If we drop the "impossible,"
then what's left is our world,
the constructs of our mind,
around which our civilization is furled.
A monster Chimera it is, all make-believe,
a fata morgana, a mirage, imagined, unreal.
But if enough people believe in it, it works.
Yet beware of thieves, lurking everywhere,
coming up with new ideas and new tools,
to steal what's constructed,
our fictions of life.
What is left will be chaos,
no more culture to share.

I don't think of all the misery,
but of all the beauty that remains.
Anne Frank

Traveler

I wanted to be a traveler,
but made it not always.
Was I then a tourist?
This name doesn't fit either,
for it wasn't my cause.
I didn't take pictures,
just wanted to see,
to sense and experience, to reverie.
This is what a traveler does.
While a tourist is chasing from place to place,
on a different trajectory,
not oft finding peace.

When we are unable to find tranquillity within ourselves,
it is useless to seek it elsewhere.
François de La Rochefoucauld

Sin

St. Augustine's Original Sin
may appear to the casual observer
as so much spin.
But there's more to it,
although ignorant about it, I am.
I'm no theologian, nor want to be.
But I've caught a glimpse
of what's there to see.
We are all fallible, like the proverbial Adam and Eve,
since we gained consciousness,
were kicked out of our animal paradise,
until then of good and bad unaware,
such as animals, innocently, are.
We are cursed to struggle between
what is good, what is bad,
between emotion and reason,
between remorse and triumph,
and Sir Galahad.

A dreamer is one who can only find his way by moonlight,
and his punishment is that he sees the dawn
before the rest of the world.
Oscar Wilde

Voices

Problems we carry from earlier times,
that haven't been voiced, aren't fully known,
remain unresolved, to be carried on.
If they aren't dealt with,
spelled out into the open,
they haunt their "owners"
to the end of their lives,
keep them prisoners of the past,
bar them from freedom,
from the freedom to strive,
for what they might yet accomplish,
become able to in life.

The big question is whether you are going to be able
to say a hearty yes to your adventure.
Joseph Campbell

Porridge

The election results of recent weeks,
of two thousand sixteen, that is,
produced surprises and thus many shrieks.
Some folks were upset and distraught
by what the future now may hold,
that which the voting has us brought.
Here's what I said,
with some folks shared:
The porridge isn't eaten as hot
as it's being prepared.

A gentleman is one who never hurts anyone's feelings
unintentionally.
Oscar Wilde

Little White Lies

are what we use
in situations we don't care to peruse.
Untruths they are,
but they help us avoid
something that's unpleasant,
or if something of interest is devoid.
They ought not to be used
except in dire need.
But note, they can be significant
used as a social lubricant.

We are so accustomed to disguise ourselves to others
that we become disguised to ourselves.
François de La Rochefoucauld

Upheaval

We live in a time when pressures grow
from scientific, technological, economic, and social woes.
The tumult they cause comes to a boil,
and the world turns topsy-turvy,
becomes awash in turmoil.
They turn some societies upside down,
chaos ensues, with luck not too long,
but quite possibly for breakdown.
Let's hope they won't happen to us now,
and we scramble back to an even keel,
somehow.

Our scientific power has outrun our spiritual power.
We have guided missiles and misguided men.
Martin Luth King Jr.

Spiderlings

glistening in the sun.
The time for spiderlings on the run,
to launch themselves into the sky,
yet sometimes it isn't quite so high.
This is, when there's little light,
to walk with the face into threads, one might.
The funny reaction is always the same,
a frantic waving of hands to reclaim
relief from the fuzziness that wasn't seen.

He who doesn't lose his wits over certain things
has no wits to lose.
Gotthold Lessing

Mindtalk

I conduct conversations in my mind
with people most dear to me,
with myself and
at times others of a different kind.
What all there is I try to convey,
alas, distance of many a kind
is keeping understanding at bay.
What is one to do when time's running out?
Write letters of the thoughts,
what it's all about?
There is so much which ought yet to be said
about issues and wishes that weren't met,
of past occurrences, of debts unpaid.
May I be given the time to accomplish yet,
that which in the following lines
by Harriet Beecher Stowe were said:
"The bitterest tears over graves are shed
by deeds left undone and words left unsaid."

Life begins on the other side of despair.
Jean Paul Sartre

Addiction

In the course of my three sciaticas
and four surgeries in three years,
I've swallowed more than two hundred opioid pills.
I still take them, when pain appears,
of my stash of one hundred
from one-and-one-half years ago.
I must still have fifty, hydrocodones they are.
Another fifty oxycodones I just had prescribed.
I suppose they will last me to the end of my life.
I am no addict, I want to be in control.
Yet deep in my mind dwells this tiny devil
that whispers at times:
Tell me what is your goal?

If you have built castles in the air,
your work need not be lost.
That is where they should be.
Now put the foundation under them.
Henry David Thoreau

Closest

The other day, my wife and I
attended a performance of the Phoenix Symphony,
when suddenly, there in the dark,
her hand moved up to touch her head.
I saw the move then heard her say:
"It is okay."
And suddenly I realized
that this woman, my wife,
I've known for decades
through joy and strife,
has been, is, and will be,
the closest human being
I've met in my life.
I've told her, I love you,
no matter, should our paths diverge,
or better yet, should they once more merge.

The best way to predict the future is to invent it.
Alan Kay

Habit

Beware of that which you repeat,
for every time you act this deed,
you reinforce this doubtful "feat."
In time this habit will become indeed
the very you beyond all need,
from which, beware, you can't be freed.

Nothing is impossible; there are ways that lead to everything,
and if we had sufficient will we should always have
sufficient means. It is often merely an excuse
that we say things are impossible.
François de La Rochefoucauld

Be good

I often bid farewell this way
to friends and people I do meet.
So far, not one interpreted my say,
the meaning I tried to convey,
the way it's meant – not morally.
Thus I must every time explain:
be simply good at what you do,
whatever it is you must see through.
What is left out, another clue,
is to yourself be right and true.

It still holds true that man is most uniquely human
when he turns obstacles into opportunities.
Eric Hoffer

Buck

There is this buck who
walks through my yard
and, of course, my neighborhood too.
I love to watch him,
always alert,
his face so lovely, so very pert.
Could I only step out
to give him a hug,
and tell him: I love you,
but our worlds are apart.
We cannot find peace
which once was a given
in paradise.

People start talking about identity
when they stop talking of what they have in common.
Eric Hobsbawm

Relinquist

All human thought proceeded
from the existence of a deity, of gods.
From the philosophy of ancients Greeks
to modern thought, atheism is a response,
the claimed non-existence of God.
It is only faith which can make one believe.
Thus, for a moment, let's suspend all belief.
We cannot know how the world was made,
so, let's start afresh,
forget who did the universe create.
If we state this position atheists we are not.
We simply claim that we do not know.
On this principle, David Hume and science go forth.
We also don't sit on a fence as agnostics have since.
No, suppose we cast the unknowable out to sea,
and "relinquish" all "unfruitful" thought
how the universe came to be.
Which need not mean that we shouldn't try to find out,
how the universe really came about.
It is the everyday world cries that for solutions,
for order and justice, for functioning institutions.

If a man will begin with certainties, he shall end in doubts;
but if he will be content to begin with doubts,
he shall end in certainties.
Francis Bacon

Conjecture

There are three realms to our world,
that which has substance like a tree
or a club that can be held.
But beware of the senses
of what can be seen, heard, tasted, and felt,
for they can betray us
if not verified but merely beheld.
Then there's what science
has measured and held
to be existing, thus compelled.
The third, the largest of the three,
is all our fertile minds conjured up to be,
which, once it started, set us free
for better and worse
to create our cultures,
our lesser or greater grands prix.

... for where the cause is not known the effect cannot
be produced.
Francis Bacon

Insecurity

In the course of time I have come across
quite a few people who carry some dross.
In their minds that is,
not excluding myself,
which gnaws at the spirit,
oft unknown to its carrier,
reaching back to early childhood itself.
A man or a woman may appear firm and assured,
yet deep down in the soul
dwells a part injured.
It breaks open when this part is touched
to make a mouse roar
or a lion snore.
Likely there are people fully secure,
but many of us are sure not as pure.

Rudeness is the weak man's imitation of strength.
Eric Hoffer

Chacun à son Goût

Each to his own taste
I've often proclaimed.
But every once in a while
a good friend of mine –
now departed for a better time –
added the word "mauvais" in response,
when the matter at hand
called for adding "bad" at the end.
While grammar certainly suffered a bit,
he, nevertheless, oft hit the nail on the head.

Man is a rational animal who always loses his temper
when he is called upon to act in accordance
with the dictates of reason.
Oscar Wilde

Progress

What all I have seen
in the course of my life,
the moon landings, the space station,
and the jet planes fly.
Then came plate tectonics,
a hypothesis no longer to prove,
but rather the opposite, to disprove.
And dinosaurs evolved into birds.
For ages antacids were peptic ulcers' bane
when antibiotics truly made bacteria wane.
Then came computers into (almost) every home,
with (almost) every ear attached to
an infamous cell phone.
And there came diodes and lasers,
now driverless cars and drones.
Glad I will be
– enough is enough –
when I am finally gone.

Doubt is not a pleasant condition,
but certainty is an absurd one.
Voltaire

Fading

I looked up two friends
of decades long,
88 and 90 years old.
Both PhDs and once smart as can be told,
now no longer fitting this precious mould.
It is a threat to watch this unfold,
one's own future to behold.
My deepest wish is not to belong
to this mental and physical fading,
to have to hold on.

Every animal leaves traces of what it was;
man alone leaves traces of what he created.
Jacob Bronowski

Jacks

At Kealakekua Bay on the Big Island of Hawaii
where Captain Cook found his end,
saw his very last day,
I once went snorkeling in this bay.
Bread hunks handed out on our boat
were fed to fish by divers afloat.
I too got a hunk, because I thought
it would be neat to dote
on the Jacks (I think) gamboling for this food.
While I held the hunk tight in my right hand,
my left fed bits and pieces to the raucous Jacks' band.
But it didn't take long for them to find out,
where the source of the food was all about.
The one-to two-foot Jacks,
in a feeding frenzy went on the attack,
on my right hand that is,
thus I quickly drew back,
let go of my prize,
and left the shark-like Jacks with no little respect
and in utter surprise.

If there were less sympathy in the world,
there would be less trouble in the world.
Oscar Wilde

IQ

I ended up with an IQ of one twenty three,
better than the average one hundred,
but not enough to really score.
Stuck in this shadow land of in-between
I tried to make the best
of what had been given me.
It irked me for the rest of my life
that I hadn't been endowed enough
to truly thrive.

If you don't get what you want,
it is a sign that you did not seriously want it,
or that you tried to bargain over the price.
Rudyard Kipling

Open Society

Our open Western society, free,
is under assault
by government and private hackers,
by false information,
by Islamic terrorists,
and our very own fault.
Of our outdated election rules,
our wrong-headed referenda,
our fear of being overrun
by cellphone-equipped foreigners,
our forgetting what we accomplished in years past,
what we take for granted,
what all we have done.
We are headed for chaos
if we don't find solutions.
Maybe out of this chaos,
lucky we must be,
a new order, stable again,
will arise for us to see.

We should manage our fortunes as we do our health –
enjoy it when good, be patient when it is bad,
and never apply violent remedies
except in an extreme necessity.
François de La Rochefoucauld

Language

Thirty sounds in the animal world
are the most there are to convey information.
Long ago as upright-walking apes
we must have had a like repertoire.
Then, later, after a few baby-months
our larynx moved lower in the throat,
the modulation of sounds became a matter of note.
In families and tribes we now could convey
a greater number of meanings, as it may.
We could agree, now beyond simple warnings,
to call a certain sound a tree,
a rock a rock, a club a club, and a bee a bee.
Then came the verbs – come, go, look, see.
The vocabulary grew, idiosyncratic to a tribe,
which led to the thousands of languages worldwide.
Soon immaterial things called for a name,
thus was born the human aim,
creating imaginary constructs, a growing game.
Until at last our world at large
is made up of images, some fleeting, some to last.
Constructs they are, nevertheless,
culture we call them,
but a long way we must still go
in our fumbling progress.

The creative person is both more primitive and more cultivated,
more destructive, a lot madder and a lot saner,
than the average person.
Frank Barron

The Dream of Reason

We, Homo sapiens,
the not-so-wise-man,
lived for uncounted ages
in the darkest of pens
of superstitions, false beliefs, myths,
and the teachings of shamans.
Just a little more than 2500 years,
there arose in the area of Classical Greece,
a series of thinkers who groped their way
to reason how the world came to be,
what it was made of,
how man ought to behave,
how he could be free,
in the process getting out from under unreason's sway.
They groped and they failed
but in their good time
they laid the foundations by which we still climb.
It is still a dream,
for reason we strive,
but emotions propel us
for better or worse.

Even things that are true can be proved.
Oscar Wilde

Fallibility

Ah, the folks who are so sure,
who reduced that which they think to know
to their model's tempting lure.
Their hallmark is rigidity,
but what about validity?
They do not take into account
that they could be wrong,
they should discount
what is to them so paramount.
Errors we are prone to make.
What may look simple but is complex
is bound to lead to a mistake.
Beware, you common man, attorneys,
doctors, politicians,
you could be wrong,
check your positions.

It is the mark of an educated mind to rest satisfied
with the degree of precision which the nature of the subject
admits and not to seek exactness where only an
approximation is possible.
Aristotle

Paradigm Transposition

Many people grow up by a paradigm, firm,
never to wonder what is meant by this term.
The firmer the model,
the more linear they are,
never questioning its correctness,
safe in their minds, no door ajar.
Yet, there happens at times
in a sudden shift or creepingly slow,
a transposition of standards
to something different and new.
It can be for the better,
but make also things worse,
for what is new and not proven,
may turn to a curse.
Beware of a paradigm, rigid and fast,
and just as much, even more so,
of a mind transposed,
to a new model recast.

Attention and activity lead to mistakes as well as successes;
but a life spent in making mistakes is not only more honorable
but more useful than a life spent doing nothing.
George Bernard Shaw

Reaction Time

Imagine how fast a bird in flight
must react approaching a twig
onto which it wants to alight.
Or a gibbon swinging through a canopy, high,
not to miss that branch he intends next to "fly."
Were our human reaction times
as fast as gibbons and birds,
we would lose fewer people on the road,
inattentive nerds.

Chance is perhaps the pseudonym of God
when he does not wish to sign his work.
Anatole France

Mit Schlag

Some Viennese, among other things,
enjoy their coffee "mit Schlag."
It readily translates to "with hit,"
but in so doing suffers a wee bit,
sounding more like a gang's idle brag.
"Mit Schlag" is a tasty addition,
a generous scoop of freshly whipped cream.
You slap it with a spoon onto your coffee
to make your coffee more "süffig,"
then watch your face come abeam.
I suggest you go for the real McCoy
and not for a commercial decoy.

There is only one way to happiness
and that is to cease worrying about things,
which are beyond the power of will.
Epictetus

Silence

A house ample and warm,
reading at night, outside a storm.
The heater turns on from time to time.
The fridge in the kitchen is adding its rhyme.
A contraction crack adds to the stillness.
The spiders are mute
and the plants do not whisper.
To the left a shadow seemingly moves,
it is the ghost of one of my cats,
gone they are, no longer in touch.
Oh, for the scent of another being,
the occasional word,
the flip of a page.
But, no, it is quiet, except for the noises
to emphasize the loneliness.

It is the way we react to circumstances
that determine our feelings.
Dale Carnegie

No more Day

You wrote your life's story
as far as it went,
under the title "One more Day…"
For twenty-four years you fought for your life,
but the time came when enough of it had been spent.
You were the most courageous human being
I've ever known.
I admired and loved you, Sabine,
for the bravery you've shown.
You took your life at fifty-three,
oh, could I only, once more,
dip into Georgian Bay of Lake Huron with thee.

Strength does not come from physical capacity.
It comes from an indomitable will.
Mahatma Ghandi

Ephemeral

For some it is three-score and ten.
For others it is a much shorter run.
When a beloved pet departs,
a friend, or worse, a family member is the one,
it drives home to us
that we are mortal,
that our days are counted under the sun.
Behold therefore what
Harriet Beecher Stowe once said:
"The bitterest tears over graves are shed
by deeds left undone and words left unsaid."

We demand rigidly defined areas of doubt and uncertainty.
Douglas Adams

Rikki-Tikki-Tavi 1

The Bard of Empire, Rudyard Kipling he was.
He wrote stories aplenty
at the height of the Raj.
One is the tale of a young valiant mongoose
who challenged the two cobras
in an English couple's garden and house.
The chittering mongoose in his Jungle Book
is the hero personified
and the chittering Rikki-Tikki-Tavi's name
has now to my new tortoise shell cat been applied.

Our characters are the result of our conduct.
Aristotle

Comets

Dirty snowballs they have been called,
kilometer-size, made of frozen gasses and water ice
with an addition of some minerals.
On a large enough pool they might actually float.
In the Oort Cloud, lightyears-far,
hundreds of thousands, maybe millions,
circle the solar system,
at times one gets disturbed by a passing star.
Or one bumps another, inward to dive,
to the inner system where we try to strive.
Old ones' orbits, like Halley's, are known.
New ones can enter from any direction
on a trajectory all their own.
They are spotted late, their speed being great.
We can only observe them
with no chance to deflect them as of this date.
Not that it's likely one will complete our fate.
They aren't like asteroids in regular orbits
we mostly know, could deflect.
No, they'd come out of nowhere, hard to detect.
So, all this talk of an asteroid hitting Earth soon
is nothing against the unlikely comet spelling doom.

Everybody wants to save the Earth;
nobody wants to help mom do the dishes.
P. J. O'Rourke

Questions

It was four centuries ago when
the Essayist, Michel de Montaigne,
sitting at his desk,
his cat joining him there,
asked the question:
"When I play with my cat,
who knows if I am not a pastime for her
more than she is to me?"
Are both conscious,
each to what extent?
I now have a cat again
who joins me on my desk.
The question I have playing with her:
Must I now write essays too?
An essay is defined as a short piece of writing
on a particular subject.
Well, my poems are short
and address particular subjects.
Ergo, I am an essayist.
An essayist of a shortish kind.

We don't see things as they are,
we see them as we are.
Anais Nin

Skepticism 1

The English write it with a "c,"
for Americans a "k" 's okay.
In my now eighty years I have become
something of a skeptic, and then some.
I'm not as profound as its Greek inventor, Pyrrho, was,
nor at all like those who came after him
who fleshed out its cause,
not calling it a position but a process,
an investigation, a search of what is facing us.
I've learned to doubt the facile answers,
the stock replies, the gut-powered response,
of which their speakers are rarely aware.
Most subjects are more complex than they appear,
thus, being too rash in assessment
can make a fool of you, I fear.
The fallibility of our thoughts
is greater than is thought by "naughts."
I, too, am very much aware
of fallibilities I had and have my share.

Sloppy thinking gets worse over time.
Jenny Holzer

Pelicans

They look like a leftover from the Cretaceous,
in flight they do not look very gracious.
But, oh, when the Browns go diving for fish,
streak for the water with great panache.
I've often identified with this bird,
it's awkwardness in flight,
yet it's dive into water
so daring, so great.
Only gannets are better at it,
but then, they are sleeker,
which helps quite a bit.

Action: the last resource of those who
know not how to dream.
Oscar Wilde

Montaigne 1

He has been described as claiming
to have portrayed himself
"naked" to posterity,
merely telling what passed through his mind
in its naked simplicity and force.
He explored his private self informally and transparently.
School-boy exercises they were called,
freely wandering through discordant subjects:
Of rabbits and trees, of politics and space,
of geology and beauty, of hope and despair.
He wrote in the first person,
peppering his essays with classical erudition
but also with personal memories and observations.
He claimed to have written "for neither you nor my own glory,
in my simple ordinary fashion,
for it is myself that I portray."

Be careful what you pretend to be
because you are what you pretend to be.
Kurt Vonnegut

Snail

Were I a snail slithering slower each day,
should I pull in my horns
or play the odds, come what may?
If I pull them in
there's less going to happen.
If I keep them extended
all kinds of things may yet come cracking,
to slither along for a few more days,
weeks, months or years,
with mind and body still somewhat in tune,
not to retire into a decrepit cocoon.

He who knows enough that is enough
will always have enough.
Lao Tsu

Chaos

There's a German saying that
"when the donkey has had it hunky-dory and nice,
he will go dancing on the ice."
Thus it is with human affairs,
when people, nations, have had it good for years,
reason defers to gut thinking,
and they put what they have in question
unthinking, without shedding tears.
Thus, after seventy years of European peace
the Brexiteers depart with cheers
with other populists playing also on fears.
Americans aren't far behind,
they may even be in the forefront of being blind.
In a couple of decades, chaos will come,
after which, hopefully, reason will trump,
without war and economic contraction
having put us in a dump.
Waves come and go with their ups and downs,
humans are so fallible, such terrific clowns.
Short is my time to see this occur,
and I'm not given the time
to see good times recur.

We often give our enemies the means of our own destruction.
Aesop

Toast

In my twenties I had an Indian friend from Kolkata.
He went by the name
Milton Surajit Kumar Guha Thakurta.
We talked and we talked of our different lands,
our different customs, our different stands.
He had studied in England
where only white toast bread he saw,
while in Germany rye was the custom,
causing him to exclaim:
"What! You eat your bread raw?"

Nothing shows a man's character more
than what he laughs at.
Johann Wolfgang von Goethe

Homo Deus

Only a Jew, Yuval Harari, could dare dream
for Man to climb heights yet to be seen.
Before we will get there
– if we ever will –
we'll see a few troughs
we need yet to fill,
or should I say:
climb some substantial hills.
My doubts are great,
although I wish he were right.
But what would we do,
if we'd gain such might?

I put my heart and my soul into my work,
and have lost my mind in the process.
Vincent van Gogh

Obsession

In the still of the night I awake,
thoughts flare, alight
on a subject sometimes important,
sometimes mundane
churning and churning through the brain.
It cannot be stilled, hard as I try,
discipline's no help,
the mind won't comply.
I need to get up
and read in a book
then head back to bed,
and wonder how sleep came so easy,
just some minutes it took.

Nature does nothing in vain.
Aristotle

Dirt

Why is it people are so very prone
to sweep dirt at the opponent's door?
Enormous progress would be shown
if dirt would be swept first at one's own.

If God listened to the prayers of men,
all men would quickly have perished:
for they are forever praying for evil against one another.
Epicurus

Yes, but . . .

How often have you sensed this "but,"
before it was spoken,
most likely originating from the gut.
The "yes" becomes irrelevant;
the "but" for the other more significant.
At times "but" merits to be heard,
its content rationally to be shared.

Only fools and charlatans know and understand everything.
Anton Checkhov

One, Two, Three

Sixty years ago it was
when an IQ test I did take.
On one of the metrics I scored low,
on some I did well, others so-so.
To my great chagrin my total score
put me on an above average, but middling floor.
I've forever grieved this passable grade,
wishing a higher mark I would have made.
To have the smarts of understanding more,
and not that some would be a chore.
Yet I can say with quite some glee
I'm able to count: One, Two, Three.

If thou will make a man happy, add not unto his riches
but take away from his desires.
Epicurus

Aurora Borealis

Fire in the Sky.
I've seen them on rare occasions,
Most are between 80 to 500 km high,
atoms of oxygen and nitrogen
giving them their colors,
purple, green, yellow and red to spy.
If only I could see once more their glory
before I die.
I would need to head north,
far, in winter's time,
for only then could I see them fiery yet sublime.
Yet as my health stands
permit me the plea
to see, this grand sight, here and there, on TV.

Experience is one thing you can't get for nothing.
Oscar Wilde

Intensity

I am of a sensitive nature,
and while some people may not concur,
I usually engage intensely
with whatever subject has come to the floor.
Yet intense engagements are so exhausting to me
that I've learned to husband my energy.
Still, if any such mental exercise is long enough
I later can't fall asleep,
the mind continuing to turn over the stuff.

Nothing is enough for the man
to whom enough is too little.
Epicurus

Equanimity

Ataraxia, Greek philosophers called it,
a state I would like living by,
alas, it's not always easy,
but I do try.
In much of my life I do succeed,
at least in these later years
as it appears.
At times intensity gets the better of me
at the cost of wasted energy.
To keep composure, to stay calm,
believe me, is a mental balm.
Altogether, as a tool,
it happily serves to keep one's cool.

Beware lest you lose the substance
by grasping at shadows.
Aesop

Priming

When I turned eighty I vowed to myself
to no longer talk ailments at great length,
when meeting with some same-aged friends.
There's nothing wrong with a brief exchange
to learn something new to help in one's way.
But if one delves too deeply, too long,
it becomes a set-up to think in ill terms, which,
is an illness by itself,
a priming that is patently wrong.

There is nothing more deceptive than an obvious fact.
Arthur Conan Doyle

Rikki Tikki Tavi 2

I marvel at the tail of my cat,
it seemingly having a life of its own,
like a separate creature
moving by itself, alone.
Sometimes I think this is what it is,
so alive by itself,
that its attached body's control
seems truly amiss.

The world of reality has its limits;
the world of imagination is boundless.
Jean-Jaque Rousseau

Montaigne 2

More and more I learn
to understand and to discern
how much this man of centuries past
is, still today, at least to me, of much concern.
He truly is a soul mate, great,
I found him only after, to this date,
I had composed eight hundred
often similar comments on the world's
and human state.

Wise men talk because they have something to say;
fools, because they have to say something.
Plato

Cat's Paw

It does not take long when I sit at my desk,
that my companion, my cat, leaps up to be next
for my companionship, to be caressed.
From behind my computer then come her paws
trying to catch my hand on the mouse,
if ever there was one that she saw.
I must respond to these playful paws,
her claws better sheathed to avoid my withdraw.
Thus I write my poetic prose
reminded of, when years in the past,
another man, interrupted by his cat,
continued to compose,
when his ink-dipped pen
scratched over his writing pad.

Question everything. Learn something. Answer nothing.
Euripides

Windy

It is windy today.
The shadows of pyracantha twigs and leaves
thrown on the top of my desk
skitter hither and yon.
What a simple, pleasant sight it is
to latch on.
To follow the shadows ever changing tracks.
At least it is sunny today, for a change.

When you look long into an abyss,
the abyss looks into you.
Friedrich Nietzsche

Departures

I'm getting older year by year.
In the recent past I have lost five friends,
some older, some a wee bit younger
and two cats, all very dear.
And there are some whose departure
– I see the horizon –
is looking ever so near.
I'm trying my best to hang on for awhile,
but the longer I hang,
the sooner my own departure will appear.

If thou wilt make a man happy, add not unto his riches
but take away from his desires.
Epicurus

Fiction

Once many years ago
there only existed objective reality,
such as a rock, a hand, a tree,
not that the creatures trotting the world
had yet names for these "things"
they were able to see.
But just like many mammals and birds
they had warning calls,
at most thirty in number,
such as for lion, hyena, and snake.
Then, here and there, one or two did agree
to give names to other things
of their objective reality.
Verbs, adjectives, and prepositions came to be
with languages evolving,
different between the tribes of the human sea.
Then, imagination took a leap,
creating subjective realty, fictitious entities, ideas,
like a bear being a deity,
from whom you begged fortune, to whom you would plea.
There arose the thought that your own people, near,
were a tribe being human,
while others beyond using different customs and words,
were not human, might become allies,
but might instill fear.

Fictitious ideas, languages, and customs grew,
like corporation, religion, and nation, adding to the stew.
And for as long as people believed
in their creation, their fictitious ideas,
they became able to cooperate, often fight,
but when once an idea felt no longer right,
such as Zeus and Athena and others of their kind,
these fictions ended up in the dustbin of history, alright.
Thus our worlds imagined are,
if rightly applied they will carry us far.
We call them Cultures,
small and large, the entire lot.
Some are better, others are not.
But change they will,
we haven't seen it all yet,
corporations, religions, and nations will crumble,
but in the meantime they will not stand still.

When smashing monuments, save the pedestals –
they always come in handy.
Styanislaw Jerzy Lec

How to Live

Through times immemorial
there are teachings afoot,
telling people how to live
for their own or their deities' good.
Today we find them in books galore
in videos, TV spots, articles, and more.
It isn't my intention to depreciate them here,
many contain knowledge and wisdom to share.
Yet, when I feel I'm told what is good for me
my hackles rise subconsciously.
I do not need gurus or know-it-alls,
for life is too complex to find a catchall.
And some that are offered
come across as a ruse,
no, I'd rather fool myself
and pick and chose.
I will make mistakes,
of this I am sure,
but I'd rather do this
then to fall for some lure.
And with all this said,
the time is now rife
to claim that variety is the spice of life.

A journey of a thousand miles begins with a single step.
Lao Tzu

Forgiving

Trying to remember life's take and give,
oddly, I do not recall anything,
I have need to forgive.
Is this because no one did me wrong,
or, when it happened,
the hurt did not linger,
but was quickly gone.
It does not pay to carry along
a pain, an injury ere been done.
Did I simply shrug off every insult and wrong,
shucks, I'm free,
or is my memory gone?

Always forgive your enemies –
nothing annoys them so much.
Oscar Wilde

Semantics

means understanding the meaning of words,
of phrases, and sentences
to appropriately speak.
Thus, when someone says:
"We all have our own facts,"
then he isn't aware of the knowledge he lacks,
that only something indisputable is a fact.
And when someone bandies the term prejudice about,
a preconceived opinion
not based on experience or reason,
when truly it is based on facts as such,
then "own facts" and "prejudicial fiction,"
so inappropriately used,
don't amount to much.

Most people when they come to you for advice,
come to have their own opinions strengthened, not corrected.
Henry Wheeler Shaw

Thoughts

When I write my little exposés,
my vignettes, my mini-essays,
the latter from Montaigne's French,
"essayer," to try, to attempt,
then this is what they are.
They are thoughts written down
before in their welter they are certain to drown.
So, dear reader beware.
They aren't truth graven in stone,
for almost never will anything human
be certain, fully known.

We can be knowledgeable with other men's knowledge,
but we cannot be wise with other men's wisdom.
Michel de Montaigne

Predictions

It was in 1959, I, at the age of twenty-three,
in Paris worked at a French company.
Two of my colleagues were communists for sure,
we argued and argued about its lure.
Yet I maintained through our spin,
telling them: Your creed isn't going to win.
Now, years have gone by
and we know how it turned out,
when a seemingly new threat is close, about.
Islamists, or Islam per se,
intends progressive life modes to flay.
Being rigid, looking backward, or to pray,
permit me to predict,
isn't going to fly.
This, for the future, I dare say.

It is folly for a man to pray to the gods for that which
he has the power to obtain by himself.
Epicurus

Dystopia

It is the year 2102,
a few years more or less won't disturb the queue,
when plenty of people will have nothing to do.
When AI, Artificial Intelligence, has completed its coup
making people redundant,
having taken over from what people once knew.
What will they do, these people, this chaff?
Taken care by the state, doing drugs,
be immersed in virtual realty,
doing yoga, meditation, seek enlightenment,
and other such stuff?
Will this be enough?
The spoils of this trend will go to a few
a new elite of knowledge, who
control the means and who knew,
in time, how to play the game,
anticipated what was to ensue.
Will there be reserves for those without clue,
to spend their idle, empty lives
like critters living in a zoo,
with AI looking after them,
their breeding controlled,
to eventually dwindle away to a very few?

Yesterday is but today's memory,
and tomorrow is today's dream.
Kahlil Gibran

Brave New World

We live in a time of increasing change,
ever faster we move.
The young live in a digital world,
politics lag behind science and technology,
thus politicians become wheely-whirled,
no longer knowing how to deal with the new
and try to fall back to the old they once knew.
But it doesn't work,
we can't return to where we came from,
some still believe it,
beware its outcome.

It is the theory that decides what we can observe.
Albert Einstein

Life vs Artifact

My not so little new cat,
just a bit over a year old,
rambunctious she is,
and lo and behold
she has already broken or cracked
four vases all told.
But life is more precious,
more precious than gold.
My beautiful Rikki was each time paroled.
I love her so much
from the bottom of my heart,
and not long ago I made her the promise,
come what may:
Only death shall us part.

One can be the master of what one does,
but never of what one feels.
Gustave Flaubert

Oxytocin

This neurotransmitter, a powerful hormone,
discharged in the brain
when a baby is breast-fed
but also during sex,
sometimes called the cuddle-hormone,
can also put on people a hex.
It produces such a pleasant rush
that some folks never get enough,
it feeling better than getting a royal flush.
For some an addiction comes to the fore
ever and ever demanding more.

Hope for pleasure is almost as enjoyable
as the pleasure itself.
William Shakespeare

Childhood

I almost forgot my first scary experience in life,
which I now enter here before the war's coming strife.
I must have been four when the son of good friends,
a Luftwaffe pilot, was home on leave.
On the spur of the moment he took hold of me, then held
me kicking and screaming over the balcony's balustrade
three stories down,
all to promote Hitler's super race, the clown!
In 1943 the attacks over Germany increased.
Americans bombed by day, the British by night.
At five I was in a hospital,
recovering from hernia surgery,
a night Wiesbaden was bombed,
with only a faint memory, if at all,
when my bed, also those of everyone else,
was rolled from the room to an interior hallway,
the only means of shelter, defense.
British air raids took place in the dark of night
and certainly caused the greatest fright
to me, an ignorant six-year-old-tyke.
American aircraft attacked by day,
my later drawings so display.
When squadrons of aircraft were on approach
an advance siren call was issued to warn.

At night, I had to be taken from my bed,
made ready for the shelter to head.
The repeated experience, the siren's call,
caused me to either poo or pee in my pajamas.
I needed a clean-up, fresh and warm clothing to boot,
then often waited for full siren warning in the living room,
where the grandfather clock did its nerve-wracking tic-toc.
At last, we headed for the shelter next door,
a dark, and scary cellar with a damp floor.
People sat quietly along the walls
waiting for the bombs to fall.
When they did, their impacts, their vibrations,
made me twice try to escape up the stairs,
out of the threatening confinement,
my dad catching me by the bottom of my pants.
After Mainz was leveled, a couple of miles across the Rhine,
my dad took me to a tall apartment's roof,
to show me the conflagration the city, her people endured.
By late summer of '44 my parents decided
that the traumas were too much for me.
Father took me away from town
to the country, a small village, Jagsthausen, family friends,
where I found peace from the war and amends.

I slept in the same bed with my cousin who snored,
so I pinched his butt to stop it,
which he promptly his mother told.
Thus an adjacent storeroom was rigged for me to sleep.
The first night was terror, almost worse than the bombings
I had escaped.
Mice kept jumping across my feather bed,
and below my sole window lots of thuds could be heard.
That they were caused by the next door farmer's sows
I hadn't yet learned.
Then, the clock in the little church rang midnight in,
this, the ghostly hour, to add to this din?
I most anxiously waited for the one o'clock ring.
We romped through the maize fields,
collected the silk, dried and smoked it,
we seven-to-ten-year-olds, unleashed kids.
One of our group was the Götz von Berlichingen son,
living in his castle, where we had the run.
Alas, he died early, is now long gone,
while I'm still around to write, "having fun."
We played on a meadow when a low-flying fighter,
roared toward us, causing us kids to wave and scream,
thinking, of course, it to be German.

But when it buzzed low over our heads,
it turned out to be an American,
the pilot, luckily, not firing his guns.
Dispatched to a sugar beet growing estate
we were taught the developing plants to properly space.
Potato beetles introduced from America
we pupils were ordered to collect.
We didn't like the goo they left
on our hands, which is why we escaped,
crossed the Jagst River up to my waist.
I couldn't swim yet at the time,
but made it across, wasn't laid waste.
Much later I watched American soldiers "fishing"
in the river with hand grenades.
In fall, when potatoes had been dug in the fields,
fires were lit at dusk to roast leftovers in the ashes,
an adventurous treat.
One night in December we were urged to wake up,
to walk out of the village, there was a rub.
We stood on the road, looked up into the sky,
which was lit from the fires of bombed Heilbronn
fifteen miles away.
In winter some of us jumped on a snow plow,
horse-drawn, which took us into the country
without proper clothing to stay warm.

Of course, we hadn't told our folks what we did,
thus we were missing for hours – inconsiderate kids!
In the last few days, close to war's end,
there arrived several German soldiers
for the village to defend.
Down by the centuries-old bridge they dug a trench
to blow up some tanks upon their approach.
The village mayor talked them out of it,
told the boys to go home,
that the war was over, the damage done.
But in a final act of defiance, a stupid one,
of the age-old bridge they blew up a span,
when a ford just below afforded a knee-high, quick crossing run.
Shortly thereafter American GIs came carefully walking
along the houses in single file,
followed by a tank column which stopped for awhile,
with the villagers and us kids watching openly or from inside.
And from a tank came flying, I caught it in time,
a small packet of chewing gum, the first of my life.
Childhood experiences all, many more could be told,
but this is enough for a haul.

Ah, except for one more, when at home again,
we played with live anti-aircraft ammunition,
took the powder out – this at the age of ten –
then put it on nearby street car rails,
to be ignited in sizzles by passing trams.
There was so much stuff lying around after the war.
We found calcium carbide,
put it in bottles, tossed them into the Rhine,
there to explode once water got inside.
We didn't tell our parents, what would they have done?
They dealt with their own problems, were too hanging on.
It must have been in '47 when life was still dear,
when I saw a body taken from the river,
a woman's, having taken her life in what was Germany.
City people suffered the worst of fate,
were short of food and in winter coal to heat.
My family was good in getting through
from grandma's grocery store – little was to be had –
to a garden where we our veggies grew.
And we lived right close to the bank of the Rhine,
where tug boats liked to dock overnight,
their barge trains anchored close behind.
The tug's captain bought at the store some stuff,
from him my dad illicitly got coal enough.

One night we hurried to the tug,
I was sent to its bunker to fill some sacks.
Thrown on a handcart we rushed up the street,
we stayed warm that winter, we had heat.
My grandma had this grocery store
to which she received before and during the war
produce from farmers across the Rhine,
past Mainz in the state of Rhineland-Palatine.
This was now cut off across the makeshift bridge
on the other side where the French now did live.
One day in '48, at eleven years of age,
I hitched a rucksack, packed some needles, thread,
buttons, and such, available in our American Zone,
and took the streetcar to that bridge,
walked across, the French always being a threat.
I visited the farmers who were known
and traded my goods for whatever they let go.
Some other time I invited a younger friend
to accompany me on another trading event.
Returning, we boarded the streetcar on the American side,
when a woman asked "where did you get this produce so fine?
And my young friend said "We begged for it,"
how embarrassed I, a trader, was!
It was the only time he was invited
to come along on this cause.

It brought to mind my mother's exhortation,
at which she pointed with one of her hands,
to the index finger of the other,
saying: "Trading the length of this finger,
beats working from its tip to the elbow,
which ever since I did follow.
I must have been twelve in '49
when I learned on my own to swim in the Rhine.
By no means was it rare to see a turd floating by,
my immune system, well, was served just fine.
A great relief ensued years later in '58
with Boeing's 707 four engine jet.
No longer did I awake at night
hearing a four-engine prop-driven plane,
the ones that had dropped bombs with all their might,
and had caused me to soil myself from fright.
Then in two-thousand-fourteen, more than fifty-six years on,
I once more in the little village church stood
and entered in the guest book that,
seventy years ago, I had rung its bell,
being pulled by its rope high to the heavens,
having been missed by bombings and live munitions,
and by the luck of the few not having been sent to hell.

One doesn't recognize the really important moments
in one's life until it's too late.
Agatha Christie

Probability

has always been on this, my mind.
There is no certainty, nothing of this kind.
With it we must deal throughout our life,
yet there are many a people
who think all's hunky dory,
that never will they encounter the knife
that cuts to pieces when the time is ripe.
Then there are those who are so sure of it,
whatever the "it" may be.
They aren't aware what may lurk beyond,
well, for as long as it lasts,
they forage happily.

An idea that is not dangerous is unworthy
of being called an idea at all.
Oscar Wilde

Dream

From a vivid dream I woke up
in the midst of night
and rose to write that not forget I might,
that I stood on some height,
gazed over a valley, wide.
Down below building went on,
everywhere, front, left and right.
It wasn't a truly pleasant sight.
But something called
to venture down,
and I started walking
while in my hand I grasped,
whatever it was, I never beheld.
And I came to a wall, a wall of earth,
before which I stood
and in anguish called:
"But I don't know what to do."
And a subtle voice replied:
"But you do, you do!"
And I lifted a layer of earth
before which I stood,
and I shoved what I held
deep into this gap, pushed it closed,
turned and looked up,

then walked out of the valley,
not to join any social sights,
but higher and higher
I carved up my path
to a nook in the rocks,
where I settled down right.
And once more did I gaze
across a world in a haze.
Then a presence walked up
snuggled next to me, tight.
A beautiful peace descended.
I no longer felt sadly bereft,
for deep down I knew
that I was loved.

Do not spoil what you have by desiring what you have not;
remember that what you now have was once
among the things you only hoped for.
Epicurus

Existentialism

There is this friend from decades ago,
whose faith moved him ever closer to God.
His God that is, and he suggests, I too,
become one of the "chosen,"
that I should be firm and not gamble so.
I finally quoted Kipling of ages past:
That "East is East and West is West,
and never the twain shall meet."
What he does not know
is that all human thought is fiction, indeed,
but there is nothing wrong, I think,
if his belief does fill his need.
Such beliefs gave rise to cultures, great,
I, too, am a product, was from it made.
Yet he lives in a world two thousand years old
when Man's universe was still narrow, all told.
I do know how enormous our Universe is,
with billions, even trillions of stars,
that we dwell in a "corner" of nature's peace,
when violence rules across the vastness of space.
Presumptuous it is to think we are unique,
of any consequence to the world we inhabit.
People, families, religions and nations fade.
We are nothing but grains of sand,
of death afraid.

But don't be depressed, my friend,
when the above you read,
for we must summon the gumption,
the strength and the courage,
to shape our lives given
for better or worse.
What counts is trying to do our best,
to fail and to rise is our legacy,
our bequest.
But this, too, is fiction at its best!

It is not the strongest of the species that survive,
nor the most intelligent,
but the one most responsive to change.
Charles Darwin

Mind-Meld 1

I've said it before,
I'd give a year of my life
to meld my cats mind with my very own.
At least for a time to learn and to know,
and convey this knowledge to all thus attuned.
To understand beyond her various meows,
to sense what she feels,
to be cat here and now.
A frightening experience it would likely be,
under control of instincts, of raw desires,
but also, I don't doubt it,
of feelings of pleasure, of pain and affection,
of many sensations possessed also by me.
But then I realized what I had said,
if the year counts from today,
tomorrow I'd be dead.

There is no excellent beauty that hath not
some strangeness in proportion.
Francis Bacon

Mind-Meld 2

It is only today that I realized
the always-having-been-present
desire to enter other minds.
Not just the obvious human kinds,
but also of fellow-creatures that come to mind.
To plumb their depths,
to fathom what makes them tick,
to understand and come closer bit by bit.
And in this coming-closer, yet to build,
a unity to be fulfilled.
I haven't yet found the cause of this wish,
but may still have some time
to probe for the source of it.

Our desires always disappoint us;
for though we meet with something that gives us satisfaction,
yet it never thoroughly answers our expectations.
François de La Rochefoucauld

Wired

Cultures assemble rules and ways
on how to relate, how to behave.
But these are manifestations mostly overt;
what are we to make of what is all too covert?
What goes on in those brains of everyone
is very different in each,
depending very much on how we are "wired,"
what turns us off or what turns us on,
what has been encoded at birth by nature
and what was added thereafter by nurture.
The lobes are different in every brain,
reacting to stimuli in ways arcane.
The nooks and crannies of every mind
are more complex and profound across mankind.
It is a marvel that we can relate,
sometimes badly, sometimes great.

The accent of a man's native country remains in his mind
and his heart, as it does in his speech.
François de La Rochefoucauld

Selfhood,

the being aware of one's identity.
It need not be conscious
but every entity, simple or complex,
must have a sense of the "I,"
or it would quickly perish, die.
And when my cat, Rikki,
quickly takes over my vacant, warmed-up seat,
I can't help thinking that she knows who she is.
And I gladly relinquish it,
knowing who's the boss,
my identity in retreat.

Forgive, but never forget.
John F. Kennedy

Bushtits

barely larger than hummingbirds are.
In winter flocks twenty to thirty strong,
dispersed in streams flutter through trees
in search of something to eat.
Watch closely, they are hard to see,
easily missed flitting from tree to tree.
In summer they split, pair up to build nests
woven of spiderwebs, moss, leaves, feathers, and grass,
a foot long, high up, suspended in trees.
Yes, so easily overlooked
are these marvelous tiny birds,
telling that there is more in nature
than barking dogs and honking geese.

Everything has beauty, but not everyone sees it.
Confucius

Beautiful

I've sometimes wondered how a forebear of ours,
an Australopithecine, naked, a Homo erectus, a Neandertal,
an early Homo sapiens, all dressed in furs, would react
were he to face a beautiful woman of today.
How would he be able to interact?
Would he be stunned, would he
dare come closer to touch and possess,
or would he find the apparition far too different,
too alien to address?
You've come a long way, modern woman,
from an earlier lack of finesse,
when not long ago
it was more a matter of dress.
And what's intended here
is to show the contrast from a time
not very far back, with far less flair.

Secrecy is the element of all goodness;
even virtue, even beauty is mysterious.
Thomas Carlyle

Exploration

There are worlds to explore,
other lands, other people, oceans and more.
These physical worlds most beautiful are,
but the interior world, the mind,
its observation and understanding,
requires traveling far,
a distance much greater than, well, Madagascar.
And what sometimes is found
must be called bizarre.
Intriguing it is, the human mind,
what makes us tick,
what makes us blind,
and, sometimes, what is it
that makes us kind?

No act of kindness, no matter how small,
is ever wasted.
Aesop

Paradigm

We live by a model
by which we see the world,
how we interact, what we believe,
the faith we hold, how we die,
and what will happen when all will be furled.
The time will come when this model turns old,
and men and women, it is hoped, across the planet
will develop a new paradigm to live by, behold.
What might it look like,
unimaginable, totally different, new?
It has happened many times before.
And I wager it will happen,
before all is done and the curtain closes,
many times more.

Support bacteria – they are the only culture
some people have.
Steven Wright

Name Giving

When I pursue the giving of names,
there's only information of names humans assign
to themselves and whatever objects
they care to identify.
So anthropocentric this is
when in truth so much deeper it goes,
for most higher creatures have up to thirty signs
by which they express what their realm entails.
A meerkat, a monkey, do have sounds,
names for snake, bird of prey, and carnivore cat.
Even crocs make sounds
which tell others of their kind
what is happening, what it's about.
Thus, the giving of names is much older than us,
vain that we are with our name-giving fuss.

Imagination means nothing without doing.
Charles Spencer Chaplin

Decision-Making

Once more I feel like addressing this task,
so difficult of some to ask.
What are the modi operandi?
Seemingly there are two styles:
One operates at once,
the other often takes awhile.
For some there's always time to do
what could be done right now on cue.
Procrastinators oft forget something is due,
or need to track back for a cogent clue.
Oh, the energy thus wasted,
and other folks left dangling high,
when a decision made right when it's called for,
the world not made to run awry.
There are the times and situations
when questions dangle high and dry,
decisions called for can't be made.
Well, then delay is quite in order,
until it's time for a good try.
Sometimes it's better not to wait
until all facts come trundling in,
for a decision to be made
with half the data still amiss.
But, trust me, I have found it calming
once indecision was dismissed.

Nothing is more difficult, and therefore more precious,
than to be able to decide.

Napoleon I

Talk 1

In years past I was scared out of my wits
to speak in public, such situations being the pits.
I was afraid I'd forget a thing here and there,
to get out of sequence,
to make a fool of myself, as it were.
Now, in my later years I've learned,
as it's called, to speak from the heart,
and found that it works
and to hell if I forget at times
a sentence, a word.
I have given talks an hour, two hours long,
and it is interesting how the audience becomes
often an amorphous, almost invisible throng.
Yet speaking with feeling,
oft from the depth of my soul,
I do reach my listeners fully, whole.
Then, when, at times, I focus on a single face,
the audience, this face and I embrace.

Men blush less for their crimes
than for their weaknesses and vanity.
Jean de La Bruyere

Promise

When I turned eighty I promised myself
that when I meet with same-aged friends,
no longer to talk about the ailments we have,
at least no more at rambling length.
A short exchange about what may be new,
the latest information, or what may have hit one of us
out of the blue.
But I've found it's not helpful to dwell on the bad,
better to chat and laugh about things
that let us rejoice and make us feel glad.

He who despairs over an event is a coward,
but he who holds hope for the human condition is a fool.
Albert Camus

Brother's Keeper

For years I've been told and firmly held,
not to give money to the chap at the curb.
He who's itinerant and begs for a few cents
likely on liquor or tobacco to spend.
But who am I to run his life?
For the dollar he gets,
while it may eventually kill him,
in the present will carry him on,
bring him enjoyment, make him survive.
Thus I've resolved to aim for a softer heart
and treat my fellow man no longer that hard.

The heart has its reasons that reason knows nothing of.
Blaise Pascal

"Mindfull"

I wonder, I wonder,
when my thoughts aimlessly wander,
when synapses on their own
shunt information back and forth,
little of which to me is known.
When I wait in an office I do not need
to handle tattered magazines to read.
Or worse, to pull my cellphone out,
to stimulate my synapses,
to babble with friends, to play a game,
to do this or that, to text,
or to find what it's all about.
There is plenty for me to daydream along,
to compose in my mind
another poem, no, not a song.
There's plenty of entertainment in my mind.
I don't need the distracting electronic kind.

The sole cause of man's unhappiness is that he does not know
how to stay quietly in his room.
Blaise Pascal

Touched

At a concert today
I heard a woman soloist play,
her violin more than 300 years old.
The talent she had, here on display,
even obvious to me, a musical ignoramus
who rarely, if ever, held an instrument to this day.
But the bravura she played with
touched me to tears,
when I deeply sensed what human beings can do,
what all we are capable of,
what, if we but try, to us can accrue.

We are told that talent created its own opportunities.
But it sometimes seems that intense desire
created not only its own opportunities,
but its own talents.
Eric Hoffer

Death

has stalked us ever since,
when, in the past, we became aware.
When consciousness increased,
drove home the point that life is final,
that death ends precious consciousness,
a loss so vast, so hard to bear.
Through time we've tried to calm this fear,
creating uncounted "life after death" subliminal spheres,
imagining transfer from the Here to the There.
And every adherent of the many beliefs
thinks that his is the only "right" one,
no matter that it is he who's being deceived.
All these beliefs cannot be right,
well, at least, they give reason for many a fight.
Man and Woman relinquish your hope,
quit fishing for life after death.
All life ever born must leave this Earth
and wherever it arose in the universe.
What consciousness tells us we've got to do,
is to live in the Here and let the There go.

Man makes holy what he believes,
as he makes beautiful what he loves.
Josef Ernest Renan

Chrysalis

A quiescent pupa, what marvel it is,
a butterfly in waiting to escape its confine,
to spread its wings and soar to the sky,
to flutter here and there,
a joy to the eye.
Humans too, a chrysalis can be,
enclosed in their shell,
unable to break free.
Oh, if only they could fracture their confining shell,
soar too to the heavens,
break their hindering spell,
and release the beauty
which inside them dwells.

There is nothing that makes its way more directly
into the soul than beauty.
Joseph Addison

Memorial

I was the last to speak for my friend,
loath I was to see towards his end.
Not being a speaker, I gathered my wits
and told the audience what I thought befits:
"I dug out my dark suit of thirty-five years ago,
it still fits very well, if I may say so.
I wear it because my friend, here and there,
enjoyed a bit of formality.
It was twenty-four years that we came to this town,
we from Chicago, he from Boston.
Fast friends we quickly became.
I later called him a polymath,
a most knowledgeable man.
And once another friend of color had died,
my astronomer-friend, born in Tunisia,
I now called my sole African-American friend.
Observing orbits of hundreds of asteroids in the Belt,
he was able to name them,
and the time came, when at Goldwater Lake,
he told our gathered group that he had named
one each for my wife and myself.
Thank you, I said, you will likely see:
That I make it to Heaven, 'tis the only time will be.

When his wife of twenty-four years died,
he felt alone and depressed,
so, talking through the woods we did stride.
But then, he found, or was it the other way around,
a new partner to brighten with, to rebound.
I had had the honor of being Best Man.
This was fifteen years ago, much too short a timespan."

The mathematical sciences particularly exhibit order, symmetry,
and limitation; and these are the greatest forms of the beautiful.
Aristotle

Somebody Home

From time to time
one sees a face
which looks alive
has depth and grace.
And instantly, like a living poem,
I know, I know,
there's somebody home.

Life reflects your own thoughts back to you.
Napoleon Hill

Perfection vs Probability

Through the ages humans have tried
to better their livelihood
which in past times
was slow and all too often by fate denied.
Science and technology
and rational thought increased perfection
and security brought.
This is incremental, easily overlooked,
by new generations taken for granted.
The foodstuffs available to the world,
the year-round food choices in stores,
the ever improving cars and roads,
aircraft safer every year,
medical treatments better but ever more dear.
Yet, in the end, we must beware,
that improvement toward perfection finds its limits,
there's no one hundred percent,
for probability is the final arbiter as it were.

Real generosity toward the future
lies in giving all to the present.
Albert Camus

Quetico

Twice we flew into Ontario's Quetico Park,
from there to canoe back to civilization.
Late summer was the best of season
to avoid the mosquitos buzzing invasion.
There were other trips paddling the many lakes
in Minnesota's Boundary Waters,
never mind the first days' aches,
portaging seventy-pound canoes
and backpacks, oh, we paid our dues.
But we drank water right from the lakes,
swam buck naked, listened to the call of loons,
cooked over small fires, the bacon azizzle,
worried a bit about bears, heard the howl of a wolf
in the light of a full moon.
The fish were tasty, the blueberries too,
there's nothing more peaceful
than paddling a canoe.

Contentment is the only real wealth.
Alfred Bernhard Nobel

Pixie

There was this petite, vivacious girl,
looking barely out of her teens.
She gracefully fluttered from client to client,
assisting other optometrists in their routine.
I could not help admiring her every move,
her feminine yet girlish mien,
which, altogether, I could only approve.
With assurance she talked of herself
personably, never aloof.
She had poise, the demeanor of a true lady,
and was surely no longer a girl
but a woman past twenty.

Grace is the outcome of inward harmony.
Marie von Ebner-Eschenbach

Hearing Aides

at their technological stage don't replace what hearing once was.
Music has become flat.
Women's voices with their higher frequencies,
have become harder to understand.
What still works best is to cup ears with hands,
about which I have no compunction
to do so in public in order to comprehend
what is being said by my vis-a-vis friend.
These days I prefer meetings of two or three,
preferably them facing me,
not holding their hands in front of their mouths,
though my lip-reading is nothing to brag about.
I do not mind for them to speak up,
it's better to understand them
than for me to make something up.
At the time of the year when cicadas sing,
when I walk below their tree,
my hearing aides start to buzz, to ring.
And in summertime evenings without them on,
the crickets' calls are totally gone.
Yet, there are times when silence beckons
for peace of mind,
when removing these enhancements provides relief.
Yet age has taken this precious ability,
nature being the ultimate thief.

A man trusts his ears less than his eyes.

Herodotus

Be doubtful about either!

H.W.

Intellectual Curiosity

What is it that makes some people
intellectually alive,
while others don't give a hoot,
of curiosity are seemingly deprived?
Surely they can't know everything yet,
especially when still young.
Why not ask questions
to no one's upset?
What is their mindset?
Do they not want to find out
what makes the world go round?
What it is that makes the other tick?
Where does he or she come from,
and in due course find another mind
with which to click?

Let no one be slow to seek wisdom when he is young
nor weary in the search of it when he has grown old.
For no age is too early or too late for the health of the soul.
Epicurus

Gone

I am of this age
when friends fade away.
Through the past three years,
six, some younger, some older,
did say their goodbye,
not to forget two dear old cats
who shared my life eighteen years to the day.
The neighborhood is changing.
New people, younger, are moving in.
I've reached out to make friends,
but most, kind as they are, do their own thing.
One, next door, a psychology prof,
is a pleasure to talk with more deeply than most.
What endeared him was his generous offer
to take in my young cat once I will leave.
So I write my comments on the world I see,
and while I stay engaged,
it's at a distance, to a measured degree.
I do have this new cat by name of Rikki.
This young being, rambunctious as she is,
I can love and behold,
although at times there's need to scold.

Love is not blind – it simply enables one to see things
others fail to see.
Anonymous

Post Partum Depression

I've finished translating another book
of three hundred pages,
two months it took.
Working two hours every day,
it proceeded apace without delay,
so that my daughters could have their way,
to learn what the War,
described in these books
– yes, there was one more before –
might have contributed in leading me astray.
And now that which was to be done is done,
having birthed another translation,
I experience what some mothers do,
post partum depression.

When a lot of remedies are suggested for a disease,
that means is cannot be cured.
Anton Chekhov

Blooming

My twelve-foot-tall pyracantha,
at the age of twenty-four,
is this season blooming like never before.
I hope it's a sign to come of many years more,
not its last attempt to produce seeds galore,
to secure its survival as a species evermore.
Had I not trimmed this bush four times a year,
it would surely have reached the respective height
of at least twenty feet, a veritable tree.

What you spend years building,
someone could destroy overnight;
build anyway.
Mother Teresa

Fear

is the companion of woman and man,
of all that is not understood.
It affects every being, like my cat,
scared by the noise a vacuum cleaner makes.
So, to stem your fear you must attempt
to make every effort to understand,
to leave generality behind,
go for the details,
or stay fearful and blind.

Nothing is to be feared, it is only to be understood.
Now is the time to understand more,
so that we may fear less.
Marie Curie

Pollution

Filth, muck, grime, sludge, and more,
not only make pollution galore.
There are the lights which dim our skies,
the stars, eternal, no longer in sight.
And the noise, the terrible noise we make,
loud music, motors running,
ignorance run amok, peace of mind put at stake.
The residues of drugs our waters spoil,
antibiotics used in excess
collect in our bodies, waters and soils.
There are chemical run-offs, industrial spills,
excreta from animal pens, the swills.
The nitrogen run-off from fertilized fields,
produce ever greater algal blooms.
So-called nanos are the latest to float
from cosmetics and infusions,
waters now hold.
There are most likely many more;
think to which you contribute or ignore.
And last not least, how could I forget,
is the plastics' scourge to which we abet.

Advice is like castor oil,
easy enough to give but dreadful uneasy to take.
Josh Billings

Dress Code

There was a time not too long ago
when formality in dress was the right way to go,
when going out to dine
or being invited by friends for good food and wine.
What has gone by the wayside
with today's casual ways is some decent attire,
replaced by oft slovenly dress.
Thus it is well when leaving one's roost
to dress up a bit
to honor one's host.

Liberty is the right to choose.
Freedom is the result of the right choice.
Jules Renard

Facts

Many people confuse fact with opinion.
A fact is something indisputable.
But beware, there's always this slippery slope,
for probability has a tendency to limit its scope.
An opinion is a judgment, a view,
not necessarily based on fact.
And rarely are opinions checked
as to whether their "facts" are truly backed.
Our minds are geared to accept
that which confirms our belief,
which unbeknownst to the believer
makes his opinion a thief,
of the truth, that is,
he or she can't see.
Yet, an opinion may very well be based on fact,
once skeptically evaluated
and always presented with tact.

The true value of a human being is determined primarily
by the measure and the sense in which he has attained
liberation from the self.
Albert Einstein

Fred

For years I've enjoyed, here and there,
an apple fritter from the Safeway bakery.
There once was a baker friend of mine
who also loved such a fritter just fine.
Thus, at times, when it fit the bill,
I picked up two fritters, then drove up the hill,
dropped in on Fred's, and we munched our fill.
Fred is gone now for many a year,
but sometimes, when I get such a fritter,
I still remember the Dear.
Then I sit in the car in the parking lot,
and while eating the fritter remember Fred,
ponder fate and impermanence,
old friendships and what not.

Life has taught us that love does not consist in gazing
at each other but in looking outward together
in the same direction.
Antoine de Saint-Exupery

Simplicity

As I've said a few times before,
most of what I write in my poetic prose,
is just a framework, no more.
The usually greater complexity I do not address.
More is left out, I must confess.
It invites the reader,
sensitive as she or he may be,
to explore further,
to access the subliminal
which is always there.
To delve into one's mind,
beyond the daily grind,
which, for survival has need,
to abstract, to simplify,
but, if not challenged,
stays simple, indeed.

The time when most of you should withdraw into yourself
is when you are forced to be in a crowd.
Epicurus

Integrity

When we think of integrity
and ask it to be defined,
we likely will propose its constituents,
such as honesty, ethics, righteousness, sincerity,
trustworthiness, truthfulness, decency, fairness,
and others coming to mind.
Yet, at its root lies the Latin "integer,"
something undivided, unimpaired, sound, complete in itself,
wholeness refined.
In a book I just read
the author ascribes to some Sudanese tribesmen,
simple folks of Muslim faith,
with little to take and little to give,
barely touched by Westernized life,
the epitome of integrity, their very being corroborative.
And beyond, the author suggests
that our so-called civilization
with everyone headed in different directions,
many captivated, endeared by electronic affections,
its members having lost wholeness,
oft hustling along without much direction,
is bare of integrity and short of reflection.

The misfortune of the wise is better
than the prosperity of the fool.
Epicurus

Skepticism 2

No matter how it's written, though,
philosophy maintains that certainty
is impossible to know.
Radical scepticism denies
that for knowledge and rational belief,
judgment ought to be suspended,
like the "big questions" of our life.
In ancient Greece a "skepticos"
was an inquirer, unsatisfied, looking for truth.
Skeptics of Old carried it too far
by claiming that nothing at all
can be known for sure.
I hold it with a simpler kind,
scientific skepticism's on my mind,
to test beliefs for reliability
and to discover empirical evidence
to probe, to question,
not to remain blind.

A definition is enclosing a wilderness of ideas
within a wall of words.
Samuel Butler

Will

It is volition, choice,
the faculty of deliberate action.
The power of choosing one's life!
Of whatever one is faced with in peace and in strife.
One can get out of a rut, leave past hurts behind,
get rich, fulfill a dear wish,
go where one must, forgive and forget,
take control of one's mind,
thus remain no longer confined.
One must be aware, want something strongly enough,
whether it's to break just a habit,
or something more tough.
Trust me, one can assume such command.
Some people can do it,
others can't.

The education of the will is the object of our existence.
Ralph Waldo Emerson

Decisions

are resolutions reached after consideration,
representing commitment, resolve, determination.
They are conclusions, choices, options,
sometimes to be made without having all information.
The worst we are faced with is vacillation.
Another one is procrastination.
Oft we must merely gather the Will
for a decision to be made,
but once done
the mind is clear, no longer buffeted,
no longer afraid.

The impossible is often the untried.
Jim Goodwin

Guns

I never ever wanted one,
never faced a situation that called for a gun,
or where I was threatened by not having one.
I may have been lucky through my eighty years,
stayed out of bad places and other such spheres.
Might it be also a question of the bearing one takes,
how one projects, the impression one makes?
To walk away from a situation too tight,
not having need to protect my ego,
instead of getting into a fight.
And I was never robbed or stolen from,
since I protect my valuables from such scum.
I wonder, I wonder what makes folks carry a gun?
Is it the society they live in
that keeps fear on the run?
In all likelihood they never had need
to make use of one.

To him who is in fear everything rustles.
Sophocles

True To Oneself

Ah, what is truth, truth of oneself?
Erikson claimed that what at old age wafts in the air
is either integrity or despair.
It means that others are not defining you
or making decisions for you to endure,
but that you make them yourself as you see fit to do.
It is integrity pure,
not its mere characteristics for sure,
but rather their entirety, wholeness, pure.
It means not chasing after some spiritual lure,
but remaining true to yourself,
to whatever you hold true.
Each of us must find this goal.
Some do, while others tend to end up on a shoal,
distraught or shallow, without much soul.
And wholeness entails respect for those
who other persuasions are likely to hold.
No matter the kind of wholeness achieved,
each serves its holder when firmly believed.

Maturity consists in no longer being taken in by oneself.
Kajetan von Schlaggenberg

Can I Help you?

More often than not
when entering a store,
one hears a friendly voice asking
"Can I help you?"
To which I respond,
to lighten things up,
"I cannot be helped!"
And we are off with a smile and a pleasant talk.
Yet there's no guarantee it will always be so.
There was a time when a sales clerk
straight-faced, with no humor,
turned, and walked away to my woe.

Whenever people agree with me
I always feel I must be wrong.
Oscar Wilde

Parchment

I do refer here to animal skin
in ancient times used for writing on.
Beware, it isn't the hide I'm referring to,
but rather the inner lining which was used in lieu.
Well, these days, my outer hide,
my animal skin,
is like this material people once scribbled on.
It's getting thinner by the year,
wounds and hematoma quickly appear.
One thing, though, has become thicker, no doubt,
issues I now can easily flout:
the very skin I'm talking about.

He who wants a rose must respect the thorn.
Persian Proverb

Backslide

Once the Roman Empire had run its course,
(like many others before, and yet to come)
exhausted, corrupt, no more plunder as a resource,
the hold on its civilization slipped, too.
And where its influence had been more distant,
the greater was the descent into chaos,
the backslide into ignorance, the Dark Ages,
the former glory a pale residue.
For centuries Europeans bootstrapped themselves,
helped by lingering memories of the past.
Oh, how long did it take to grow into its own,
for new nations to arise,
how much strife, how many wars had to be lost and won?
Exhausted after two global wars
and with the help of America,
they forged a peace lasting seventy years.
But now they and their benefactor
forget the good it was they wrought,
question what all they were given,
longing anew for the shedding of tears.
What is it in the human mind
that, as time passes,
to the past, but to the future, too,
we become blind?

Decay is inherent in all compounded things.
Strive on with diligence.
Buddha

Perpetrator

He or she who harms is an aggressor.
This is how it is commonly understood.
However, he or she who acts the victim
is just as much perpetrator for his or her
or others' good.

Education is the ability to listen to almost anything
without losing your temper or your self-confidence.
Robert Frost

Buddha

Siddharta Gautama was born a prince,
known as The Buddha ever since.
He left his well-off abode in India 2500 years ago, hence
to acquire wisdom and teach it as a consequence.
Myth tells that in his pursuit he barely slept,
ate only a grain of rice a day,
and slept on nails for a bed.
Thus he is venerated,
must have been skinny as a rail,
Then why is he pictured across Asia
in full-fleshed glory, oft even chubby,
bringing some weight onto scales?
I don't doubt that he had something to say,
but pardon my irreverence,
it's not my intention anyone to sway.

The misfortune of the wise
is better than the prosperity of the fool.
Epicurus

Pebbles

Tumbled and ground in rushing rivers,
in the surf of ocean shores,
carried to where they are nowadays found
in thousands of years from rocks afar.
They come in all sizes and colors galore.
But pebbles are small,
might they have been boulders before?
Used on pathways and walls as decor.
To Arabs with cool water running across,
they became a foot-massaging, soothing floor.
Across the world pebble beaches are found.
One I recall in Oregon, standing out.
The noise of the churning pebbles is loud.
Their colors are varied.
If the tide is right, some agates may be found.
Once, on a misty morn, with my daughter along,
we scoured the beach, but the tide was wrong.
No agates turned up, but the colored pebbles
were inducement enough
to chuck her poncho, no matter the mist,
and carry a good load of colorful pebbles off.

Forgiveness is not an emotion, it's a decision.
Mahatma Gandhi

Rikki Tikki Tavi 3

I had need of a companion,
now half a year ago,
so I went to the Shelter,
where it was love at first sight,
when I Rikki found.
She scratched at the window
of her small plexiglass bin,
and I knew I had to take her to add to my kin.
Just a year old but fully grown,
some people had adopted her
but had returned her again soon.
As it turned out they likely couldn't deal
with this vivacious youngster's zeal.
She was wild and rambunctious,
two days in my home,
she raced up the trunk of a Madagascar Palm,
toppled it, broke three branches,
almost caused the tree's doom.
I checked her paws, there was no sign of hurt,
that could have been caused by the spiny bole.
In the first four weeks four vases she broke,
I didn't mind, took it as a joke.
By now she has settled down a bit,
no longer scratches and bites.

And for attention she rolls on her back,
saying "pet me, pet me," which I like so much.
And we talk a lot with each other and such.
To describe what this beautiful creature looks like,
here goes: All her paws,
her bib and her belly are white,
yet her back is mottled,
brown, orange, red, black, and grey,
a melange of colors, like a tortoise shell, it might be.
Her sides and her tail are beautifully striped.
All in all, it is difficult to assign her a type.
Thus, I am calling her, no matter what,
my beloved, tail-heavy Tortie Cat.

The more you judge, the less you love.
Honore de Balzac

Turds

In years past, when we traveled abroad,
we left our indoor cats in the care of a ward,
who came daily to water and feed the two,
but after a few strokes would again depart.
It so happened upon some of our longer trips
that, coming back, we found a turd
smack in the middle of our bed.
What went on in the mind of Spunky-cat,
for she must've been the one to deposit the scat?
Abandoned of company she must have felt,
wondering how to express her displeasure,
and, short of wrecking something,
leave a reminder that smelt,
this in the most obvious place
to be seen and beheld.
I marvel about what went on in the mind of this cat
that went from A to B, then C?
Not that it was reasoning, nothing like that,
but, starting with a feeling of loss,
led her to do what she did.
There's little forebrain in a creature like her,
yet she expressed her displeasure
in a most potent way.

It is better to fail in originality than to succeed in imitation.
Herman Melville

Rituals

I've always abhorred them.
They try to fence me in.
A series of actions performed in a prescribed order.
It can be the singing of a national anthem,
Christmas, or birthday parties,
the mouthing of loyalty spiels,
the swearing of oaths and table prayers,
church services, the bowing of hundreds of Muslims.
I have had the dubious liberty of never being able to vote.
All of the above attempts to usurp freedom,
against my desired spontaneity of expression
arising from a deeply felt commitment
to an issue, a cause,
from the wellspring of my being
and from the very moment of seeing.
Thus I quote in my Volume 1:
"When the Tao is lost there is Goodness,
When Goodness is lost there is Kindness,
When Kindness is lost there is Justice.
When Justice is lost there is Ritual.
Ritual is the Husk of Faith and Hope
and the Beginning of Chaos."

Long years must pass before the truths we have made
for ourselves become our very flesh.
Paul Valery

Information

We are flooded by it,
and it will not decrease.
And the more there will be,
the more our isolation will increase.
For when overwhelmed by information,
our instant demand
is to simplify and select
that which we like, the rest to disband.
Then we ally with those of like grandstand,
and make enemies of all those,
perceived not sufficiently grand
since they do not hew to the proper stand.

Happiness is the perpetual possession
of being well deceived.
Jonathan Swift

Serendipity,

an event happening in a beneficial way.
A happy chance, a fluke, providence, or fortuity.
In short, Fortuna's luck, come as it may.
Might this be akin to a blind date?
Are we not masters of our fate?
I grant, luck plays a role, at times,
like being in the wrong place and time,
which then is called 'bad luck,' to rhyme.
So, while I allow for Fortuna's gift,
my philosophy takes a different drift.
There are people who know what to do
and what not,
their timing being more succinct,
their approaches sometimes vague, sometimes distinct.
But people on good terms with Serendip
don't hold what they think close to their chests,
but spread their word for contacts to link.
For there lies the secret,
at least in part,
for serendipity to be more than art.

There is no more miserable human being
than the one in whom nothing is habitual but indecision.
William James

A Grain of Rice

There was a time sixty years ago
when I became friends with Tony Soon Ho.
In Paris it was at the Alliance Française,
where we tried to learn French
for better or worse.
Singapore was Tony's home.
He had studied in England,
and after learning French
wanted to add German to his language tome.
Thus he later stayed with my family for some weeks,
one day cooked for us a Chinese meal.
In its course he told of a Chinese proverb that:
"Every grain of rice not eaten from one's dish,
is going to bring a year of bad luck."
While I'm not superstitious,
I understand what by it is meant,
I have honored my disappeared friend,
by always eating the last grain of rice on my plate.
When I visited Singapore in nineteen-ninety-one,
I tried to find him in the telephone book,
but there were oodles and doodles of Ho's,
and in all likelihood he had moved on.
Yet I keep thinking of him
whenever the last grain of rice on my plate is gone.

A proverb is no proverb to you
until life has illustrated it.
John Keats

Vacillations

It's not really that I vacillate,
but I reserve the right to change my mind
whenever I feel it is opportune,
or situations have changed, as they very well might.
Thus, when I state that I'll stop writing poetic prose,
my current poor trickle of new ideas
may change once more to a flood of those.
Alas, how much more can one cogently state,
when almost a thousand are on one's slate?
Well, we'll see how things turn out,
whether I come up with some more to babble about.
And this doesn't apply only to poetic prose,
but to any subject I so choose.
And, come to think of it:
I don't give a hoot,
should others see me fickle-minded,
when changing my mood.

Words are, of course,
the most powerful drug used by mankind.
Rudyard Kipling

Memories

Having lived with a woman for fifty-plus years
and known her for ten or so more,
memories pleasant and sad piled up,
a plentiful, uncountable score.
When no new ones can be added to this store,
what is left is to dwell on what was.
And the choice must me made
on which one's to dwell,
the nice ones or the bad?
It is my decision to value both,
but to remember the good ones well
and cherish what I was given
until the toll of the bell.

Nostalgia is a seductive liar.
George W. Ball

Ever has it been that love knows not its own depth
until the hour of separation.
Kahlil Gibran

Alone

can mean being in misery
when companionship is dear.
It appears that women are better than men
in maintaining a spirit of good cheer.
Oh, were there only one to care,
in making life more worthwhile,
have someone willing to share.

What you really value is what you miss,
not what you have.
Jorge Luis Borges

Twitter

What have we come to that it seems fit
to run a country by Twitter bits?
How low have we sunk in the USA
that its policy is announced the Twitter way?
Should not the President of the USA
stay above the common fray,
keep his decisions more at bay,
and announce what's to be done
following a thorough assay?
Ah well, there will surely come the day
when enough is enough
and sane politics will be conducted again
without too much of the now common foul play.

An angry man opens his mouth
and shuts his eyes.
Cato the Elder

To Spin a Yarn

I have tried to write fiction,
to spin a yarn,
but found that I lack the wherewithal.
Am I short of the fantasy
required to delve into people's minds?
But this isn't the case,
I think I do know the buts and ifs of the physical world
and that of man- and womankind.
Thus I keep writing my poetic prose
and deal with human affairs in this way.
I'm just too factual, not an embellishing guy.

If you must love your neighbor as yourself,
it is at least as fair to love yourself as your neighbor.
Nicolas de Chamfort

Customs

It was in my early teens
when I first was aware
that I chafed at some customs
for which I did not care.
Why that was so I have no idea.
Was it just my age, had I not lived up to expectations,
that I rebelled against what held no cheer?
Not that I was myself up to anything good,
when I wanted to change
an assortment of customs and behaviors
as they stood.
Do away with the silly Christmas tree,
and while at it, the superfluous God,
no taboo about nudity,
and sexual mores ought to be set free,
a wedding ring was no longer to be.
In short, do away with authority.
Much I kept into later life,
but late only did I understand
that one cannot simply do away
with what society has ruled as normal
and what other ideas it has banned.

Our deeds follow us, and what we have been
makes us what we are.
John Dykes

Journeys

It's now eighty-one years
on my journey through life,
and to many places I've been.
Plenty of others are there still to go,
but a few I wouldn't care to see.
India and China are of this kind,
Venice is another which comes to mind.
They have much to offer,
but I don't care for crowds,
I have usually preferred places
with less noise, not too loud.
And wasn't I lucky to have still seen the world
before all too many tourists
made a shambles of the sights I was wont to behold?
Thus I booked myself for one more jaunt,
a little cruise to the "end of the world."
The Marquesas Islands are out of the way
where few people are wont to stay.
Yet they were the haunts of Stevenson,
Melville, and Gauguin, and others escaping crowds.
The date to depart is awhile yet to go.
A human child could well be born, if that be so.
But it's something I look forward to
and with a little luck I'll be healthy enough
for this journey not to fall through.

Dost thou love life?
Then do not squander time, for that is the stuff life is made of.
Benjamin Franklin

Hoax

Not long ago I met a man
over some tidbits and a beer.
I happened to mention global warming
in the ensuing conversation,
not that I wanted to raise a ruckus,
it was just a thought that had come to me.
And the fellow shot back
as if stung by a bee:
"It's a hoax, of course. Can you not see?"
By no means did he mean it to be humorous,
rather as a malicious deception, a set-up, a fraud.
But when I then probed his knowledge
about the science and facts,
the melting glaciers, the rising oceans,
and what all else had by now been checked,
he didn't know a single thing.
Thus, of ignorance he did not lack.
People, blind, are stumbling on,
nothing whatever can make them see.
For nothing can happen that's not allowed to be!

Science denial is nurtured by the false notion that democracy
means that 'my ignorance is just as good as your knowledge'.
Isaac Asimov

>nicht sein kann, was nicht sein darf!<
From *Palmström* by Christian Morgenstern

Preferences

A well-off friend, still traveling fancy and far,
then emails his pictures.
Too many they are.
His friends, anyway, receive lots of stuff,
but too polite, will not tell him: "It's too much."
But the pressure is there.
What are they to do?
I've told him the truth:
Less would be more.
Besides, my preferences these days are,
to sit late in September,
when mosquitos are rare,
by the side of a pleasant Canadian lake,
with a Scotch in hand,
and contemplate.
Listen to a loon's haunting call
nothing fancy and not far at all.

Long years must pass before the truths we have made
for ourselves become our very flesh.
Paul Valery

Outsider,

I've been at the best of times.
Insider when I write my rhymes.
Haunted by this "standing aside,"
when others had fun,
I wasn't along for the ride.
There's always this sense
that I do not belong,
that I'm somehow different,
that something is wrong.
Even when among friends
it makes for a lonely
individualistic stance,
in life's ever so complex dance.

Not all who wander are lost.
J.R.R. Tolkien

Vertigo

For weeks now I deal with vertigo attacks.
Believe me, dear reader,
as the saying goes: It sucks!
When the world turns topsy-turvy,
when you can't do a thing,
just sit where you are,
are alone in your misery,
call on friends, here and there for something to bring.
When nausea strikes to lead to a puke,
when a cold sweat pursues you,
it's impossible to walk to the toilet or to bed,
so you grope your way along walls
or on your hands and knees
to get to where you still have the need.
It gets worse when you've done all the treatments there are,
which aren't that many and none apply.
When the doctor tells you: "No more can be done.
Just hold on. It's going to pass in the long run."
It takes half a day to recover from an attack,
then another half still feeling out of whack.
I've applied the Epley maneuver, took an MRI,
leaving, maybe only Meniere's desease.
But believe me, dear reader, it is more of a curse.
Or might I be dealing with a fourth unknown cause,
forbid, maybe something worse?

The only antidote to mental suffering is physical pain.
Karl Marx

Keeping One's Word

I often promise my Rikki-cat
that later I will take her out for a walk,
about whose excitement she's apt to talk.
It's not so much about keeping my word to a cat,
but rather to myself.
And that is that!

Virtue is not left to stand alone.
He who practices it will have neighbors.
Confucius

Primeval

Tourists flock to Venice and Paris,
to London, Rome, or go on a cruise.
And while I have gone to some of these places,
I preferred being away from the madding crowd,
which all too often is noisy and loud.
To get away from civilization
– but not too far –
into nature, resplendent, still somewhat raw.
Thus there is always the call of Africa.
Her braided streams, her veldts and savannas,
where solitary acacias, cropped by giraffes
to an umbrella shape, so very characteristic,
their silhouettes at Africa's dusty sunsets, eons old,
oh, so gorgeous, to behold.
To fly to a camp, way out in the bush,
with the accoutrements of civilization
– even a toilet to flush –.
To find the company of ten or twelve folk,
join some on a game drive by day or night,
canoe a river past hippos and crocs,
or, on a bush walk come face-to-face with buffalo,
cheetahs, or waterbucks.
Where I'll be, although unlikely,
potentially be carnivore meat,
or trampled by an elephant's feet.

Then have a good dinner, a drink by a fire,
called bush-TV,
and chat with others what there was to see.
Some may now say: This is primeval light,"
But it takes me back to my genetic past,
to a time of my soul, I care not to miss,
could repeat on and on,
which the heart of a city never can.

Man is a make-believe animal –
he is never so truly himself as when he is acting a part.
William Hazlitt

Ruaha

I watched a couple of TV shows
on lion prides in Tanzanianas Ruaha Reserve,
crossed by the trickle of a river of like name.
It brought back a memory of two-thousand-fifteen,
when I stayed at Kigelia Camp right next to this stream.
Upon my arrival I was ensconced in an outlier gazebo tent,
where I quickly slumbered off when a noise awoke me a mite.
Looking up, there, not a yard from my abode,
stood an elephant parallel to my tent,
pulling down some verdure, looking quite content.
I watched the big tusker, enjoyed his company,
but when later I walked into camp,
its boss moved me closer to the camp's facility,
away from the wandering elephant,
to a tent right close to the river's wash,
a place of assumed greater tranquillity.
Later that night until I fell asleep,
I kept hearing the raucous roar of beasts,
of distant lions, there was no need to get tense.
I had a good sleep but at five in the morn,
in the wash below, right before my tent,
a mighty roar arose from a King of Beasts.
No wake-up call at the camp was required that day,
no, definitely, not the least.

My aim is to put down on paper what I see
and what I feel in the best and simplest way.
Ernest Hemingway

I Love You,

is so hard for many a man to say,
except when he's in love with a woman.
But his children, his kin, need to hear it too,
yet he is of a past generation,
when even this sentiment is felt,
there is hesitation, and back it is held.
There's always the feeling that its too frequent use,
diminishes the words, leads to its abuse,
or becomes a routine, just blabbed to make sure,
the recipient may barely hear any more,
a term to which he or she becomes inured.
With deeds I'd rather express this sentiment,
which, if properly understood,
are just as relevant.

We live, not as we wish, but as we can.
Menander

Delaying

"Oh, there's time to do what needs to be done,"
thus is the mantra of many a man,
or, come to think, of women, too,
who will likely forget what they ought to do
right after they promised
to keep their promises true.
What's delayed may never come to pass,
some is forgotten, some turns into a cloud of gas.
"Did I do this already, or did I not?"
"What was it I promised?"
"Where's my note?" "Who did I promise it to?"
"Was it to myself or what?"
Some folks delay and forget early in life.
For avoiding it some never strive.
In later years it becomes ever more rife,
forgetting, that is,
which is why it's important to do right away,
what ought not be delayed
in order to keep failed promises at bay.

You don't understand anything until you learn
it more than one way.
Marvin Minsky

Worship,

the adoration of a deity, a power, a greatness,
the reverence for the sublime.
The glorification of, the devotion to the initial three,
implies a superior force,
and, last not least, a smidgen of fear.
It is the sublime which captures our mind,
of whatever its nature,
it elevates while it humbles,
it is awe-inspiring, it's divine.

How glorious it is – and also how painful –
to be an exception.
Alfred de Musset

Indifference

We run our lives, so many of us do,
with the nose to the self,
the grindstone, too.
We have neighbors and friends,
get together and talk,
eat, drink, and ponder,
but in the end, I wonder
if any grok?
Relations are frozen
in an oft mindless task,
there's no going beyond,
for a drop-in, a call.
Are people so contained in their very selves
that few care little
beyond themselves?

It is not easy to find happiness in ourselves,
and it is not possible to find it elsewhere.
Agnes Repplier

Pressure Differential

There was this good lady,
short of some ink,
for her Brother printer it was, I think?
It was black that was called for,
by no means pink.
She pulled the tab on the cartridge as told,
but the "bullet's" charge had been placed
close to sea level's hold.
Prescott, my hometown, is a mile or more high,
and without warning, it caught her cold.
The accident was a horrid mess,
but before all was done she looked as if
she had tried to make love to an octopus.

Life is not a spectacle or a feast; it is a predicament.
George Santayana

Exuberance

When folks get to see an animal in the wild,
a deer, a javelina, a bobcat, they might,
most get so excited, they cannot hold still.
They jabber and gesticulate,
engrossed by their thrill.
They aren't aware that the ruckus they raise
will cause the creature they wish to see
to bound off as if being chased.
Ignorant, they fail to be quiet,
to enjoy that which they want to observe.
Ah, awareness, awareness!
They haven't a clue.
Their exuberance "kills the goose,"
they just don't know what they do.

The mark of a good action is that it appears
inevitable in retrospect.
Robert Louis Stevenson

Waiting

Many kinds of waiting await us through life.
There's the doctor's office,
the exam, the job application,
a confinement, the flight or train connection,
dealing with incompetence to get something done,
the delayed food order, the sleepless night,
all tax our patience, as well they might.
Some are quite similar,
but others are not.
All depend on the personality of he who waits,
how fearful he is, how rushed she is,
how he values himself when being put upon.
Confinement's depression,
the toss and turn through the night,
being made to wait considered unjust, not right.
What comes into play in this "waiting game,"
is equanimity, stoicism, composure,
endurance, resolve, and more, as the aim.
And at times, when possible,
to give hell to those we ought to blame.

There is nothing so easy but that it becomes difficult
when you do it reluctantly.
Terence

Rigmarole

In their pursuit of profit and growth,
capitalist industry, never sloth,
comes up with incentives to further both.
There are the teasers of discounts,
of a bonus, a free ticket, coupons,
a free flight, or, maybe an extra night.
I don't think I've covered them all,
but then, I don't care to play their ball.
I obtain what I need or may get what I want,
no matter the bidders' cheerful rant.
I don't care for their offers, their rigmarole,
to establish another password, to get my data,
if they could, catch my soul,
which, to me, isn't worth playing the sucker's role.
Because, at the end, there's always that
they want my money,
no matter what.

And from the discontent of [one] man
the world's best progress springs.
Ella Wheeler Wilcox
[one] removed by H.W.

Lottery

When young I challenged Fortuna a few times,
not knowing much yet, thinking big to win.
Roundabout, I was to learn
that to beat the odds is only to yearn.
In order to get where you want to go
requires to get off your bun
to properly work with a decent plan.
While I firmly believe in probability,
that in a lottery win isn't the one.
For years now, when the subject arose,
I claimed playing the lottery meant
"the taxation of the poor."
Should you, dear reader, try Fortuna's luck,
think that some of your money
will serve a good cause.
Myself, I'm just not a gambling man.

One is never more on trial than in the moment
of excessive good fortune.
Lew Wallace

Company

I enjoy the company of men,
of women even more.
With my father, remote,
both grandfathers gone,
I grew up among women,
all strong, as previously told.
While men have a need to protect their Self,
women are more personal, direct.
Men tend to speak of subjects as if
taken from a wooden shelf.
Talking about sex, women can be raucous;
men are more coarse or oft cautious.
There are times, however,
when I prefer the company of men,
when the give and take is measured.
At others, I'm quietly turned off
when women's babble gets just too much.

You cannot teach a crab to walk straight.
Aristophanes

Discussions

For many years I've gathered with friends,
rotating through our homes,
sometimes with one, two or three,
over some tidbits, coffee or tea.
We will pick any subject,
except personal ones.
Beyond these "protected" areas,
regrettably so, all others are open, considered free.
We solve all the problems afflicting the world.
Often, I've told outsider friends:
"Watch, come the following day
we'll have all problems facing us
straightened out, no more dismay.
Ah, were it only that simple to do.
Yet, here and there, we truly do learn,
come up with an insight,
or at least find some clue.

Most of the important things in the world
have been accomplished by people
who have kept on trying when there seemed
to be no hope at all.
Dale Carnegie

Cumulus Clouds

Magnificent, these puffy, oft pregnant clouds,
sometimes portending of thunderheads, rain,
but usually telling of fair weather's reign.
Illuminated by the sun like cotton they seem.
I recall a flight, years in the past,
when the view out my window
of the sky far and wide
was dotted by banks of cumulus clouds,
so beautiful,
they brought tears to my eyes.

We live in a rainbow of chaos.
Paul Cezanne

"Essayer,"

French for trying, to endeavor,
to venture, attempt, or aim.
The "essai," invented by Michel de Montaigne,
more than four hundred years ago,
served him to explore
himself and also humanity's lore,
so full of misery galore.
Like him, I try to draw you in, dear reader,
by didactic poetry, or, what I call
my brief poetic prose.
I dare to compare myself with this great writer,
more erudite than I'll ever be,
by also attempting to instruct with what I expose,
often supporting my arguments using aphorisms
from antiquity and times more close.
I try to talk straight, be honest and frank,
while being fully aware that in my own past,
when I look back, I am aghast.
But here and there, as they come to mind,
I try to sprinkle my scribbles by a poem
of lighter kind
to bring a smile to your face, if so inclined.

By three methods we may learn wisdom:
First, by reflection, which is noblest;
second, by imitation, which is easiest;
and third by experience, which is bitterest.
Confucius

Event

It was a sunny, autumn morn
when I sat with Rikki, my cat,
on a rock outcropping in my backyard.
A doe jumped suddenly from the bushes,
stopping only a couple of yards from where we sat.
All three of us stayed stock-still.
While the deer looked at the two of us questioningly,
the wind blew favorably for me and my cat.
For the longest time we eyed each other,
Rikki peeking out from behind my back.
Her tail, if it twitched, hidden.
Her tortoise color and my garb
blending in with the rock.
At last, the doe saw the strangeness of us,
turned, and leaped back into the bushes,
the boulders, and the waving grass.

Imagination is a poor substitute for experience.
Havelock Ellis

Staying Power

Not far from Crater Lake,
at the Rogue River Gorge Park,
the forest of coniferous trees
has left its mark.
Near the rushing waters
some trees once cut,
flat-topped their stumps,
maybe two feet high max.
A marvel I saw there like never before,
for the tops of the stumps,
tenacious, persevering,
were alive, solidly covered by bark,
life encore!
A ranger explained
that the roots of surrounding trees
entwined as they are,
kept the stumps alive,
having covered their scar.

From such crooked wood as that which man is made of,
nothing straight can be fashioned.
Immanuel Kant

Factual

When getting together, maybe two or three,
among the various subjects discussed,
we may talk about someone else
who isn't here.
I, for one, have no reservation
to address an absent-one's trait,
as long as it's factual
and not disparagingly made.

It is the Vague and Elusive.
Meet it and you will not see its head.
Follow it and you will not see its back.
Lao Tzu

Talk 2

To give a talk,
nightmare it is,
cause for many people to balk.
Anxiety flares,
it's so easy to stumble,
not literally, but for the words to fumble.
If the subject that's talked of
is new, even known,
if the speaker is worried
that he'll speak out of context,
that he might forget
what he should have said earlier on,
then anxiety holds the speaker back,
compared to the one
who can speak at a crack,
of that which he knows,
most fluent and smart.
The reason being:
It comes from long practice
or from the heart.

Style is the dress of thoughts.
Philip Chesterfield

Devastations

The more we become,
now seven-and-a-half billion strong,
the more we must expect
something to go wrong.
Ever more numerous we gather in cities,
many of which are near the sea,
where the waters will rise,
swamping the shores, driving many inland,
from devastation to flee.
And the rains will increase to flood the land,
where too many have built
and no levies will withstand.
The earth will keep quaking
to topple buildings, cracking sewers and roads.
Tsunamis will happen from various causes.
And to the too many
no matter how hard we try,
devastations will happen,
and many will die.

That which seems the height of absurdity in one generation
often becomes the height of wisdom in the next.
John Stuart Mill

Rules

The further in time we are going back,
the fewer rules there were to interact,
whether between people living side by side,
or those who by happenstance met.
As groups grew larger
there arose rules on how to act
in battle or trade,
although it was still a fact
that, according to Hugo Grotius' law,
four hundred years ago,
might still made right.
In the meantime we've added
plenty of rules by which to abide,
and no matter the troubles we still cause,
the times we live in
have become more secure
when these rules are applied.
No matter that groups still act uncivilized, raw,
these rules enacted and enforced
become universal human law.

Good people do not need laws to tell them to act responsibly,
while bad people will find a way around the laws.
Plato

Time

The half-acre I've owned for a few piddlin' years
holds a plenitude of boulders,
of granite, that is,
which coalesced in the interior of Earth.
Runoff from rains exposed these boulders
for erosion to eat away, to start.
They range in size from a foot to yards,
some split from larger ones into smaller parts.
In my mind I reconstruct
how they once fit together,
how they fell, where they lie,
where they were cracked by the weather.
Where lichen, varied and pretty,
age-old symbiotes of algae, bacteria, and fungi,
ate into the rock.
Where water seeped in,
then frost pushed the pieces apart.
Where I now reconstruct on how they dropped.
Smaller and smaller these pieces become
so that in time, uncounted,
boulders become sand,
and the mountains and hills
into valleys and plains succumb.

Everyone takes the limits of his own vision
for the limits of the world.
Arthur Schopenhauer

Sentiments

Many a card is writ throughout life.
Today, commercialized, picked up in a store,
all too often more dead than alive.
This excludes the ones carefully chosen,
which hit home, do not read as if they were frozen.
Then, there are the ones composed by a mind
and penned by hand,
making the content of such a card,
a sentiment coming truly from the heart.

Beauty, more than bitterness,
makes the heart bleed.
Sara Teasdale

Lamarck

Before Darwin published his Theory of Evolution
Jean Baptiste Lamarck proposed
that acquired characteristics can be inherited,
such as giraffes getting longer necks
by stretching them to ever higher leaves.
What comes here to mind,
had the man been correct,
is that thumbs of future human generations
will become ever more dexterous
from their cell phone operations.

Change is the process by which the future
invades our lives.
Alvin Toffler

Deities

Once more, here I go, how,
through thousands of years,
the variety of gods was created by Man!
With, surely, many more yet to come.
But every believer of every persuasion,
thinks that his or her own is the only true one,
and that was given to them by their god,
but not created by fallible Man.
It is the fear of death, loss of consciousness,
and the need to hold people together,
which caused Man to create "birds of a feather."
Only faith makes you think you truly know,
whatever you believe with such ardent glow.
Without commonly held beliefs,
not just religious ones, societies would fall apart.
For if everyone would hold an individual belief,
such a society's life expectancy would likely be brief.
Why do we work so hard to avoid death, our grief?
And why would a god create Man
with spinal stenosis and sagging arches?
He or She, or might it by It,
could have picked a better design from its kit.
No, the monotheists created god in the image of man.

Were we to know what other designs
might dwell in the vast universe,
ignorant to believers, made by a different plan,
would the redeemer have shown up there as well?
Oh, people, people, believe what you want,
if it serves you in life, be it not a taunt.
Its alright to have faith,
but don't push it on others,
who don't have this wont.

There is no god like one's stomach:
We must sacrifice to it every day.
Yoruba Saying

Good Laugh

What makes a good laugh,
uproarious, unrestrained, rollicking, wild,
is, when, perchance,
you almost wet your pants.

Occasions are rare; and those,
who know how to seize upon them, are rarer.
Mary Wheeler Shaw

Resigned

I am on the board of an association
whose members assemble from time to time,
to provide its functions with reason and rhyme.
With my hearing going from worse to worst,
I most often catch only half what is said.
And with my hearing aids of little aid,
intelligent comments become mislead.
Thus, before my comments become too sublime,
I think it is better I pack up and resign.

It is the way we react to circumstances
that determines our feelings.
Dale Carnegie

HERBERT WINDOLF

Save the World

Four of us friends meet once a month
at one of our homes
to discuss what's going on.
We pick various subjects,
some urgent, some not,
and try to find solutions
for the sorry lot.
Oft I have told friends outside the group,
that we try finding solutions
to the world's, oh so messy affairs,
and succeeding at it,
that on the following day
– watch out for it –
there's less trouble
and cleaner air.

The course of true anything does not run smooth.
Samuel Butler

Fancy

There are things to do, I'm certain, you fancy,
thus I tell my friends old and young:
Better do them while you can!
For the time will come
oft sooner than later,
when what you wished to do,
its opportunity will be gone.

Youth is a blunder; Manhood a struggle;
Old age a regret.
Benjamin Disraeli

Playing with Language

It is fun to confer the meaning of a word
to one a bit absurd,
not previously heard,
especially when the content transferred,
contains a plenitude of implications
which are covertly referred.
After more than five decades
in the North American realm,
I'm still German,
the origin hard to shed, to overwhelm.
But having made two cultures my home
I draw on both,
which is why, for example, I love to claim:
"I have been corrupted by American culture,"
it just happened, it wasn't my aim.

There is an art of reading, as well as an art of thinking,
and an art of writing.
Isaac Disraeli

Sights

In front of my window
a broad valley crosses my sight.
It gently rises south to the right.
A low ridge bisects it,
in front of the Bradshaw Mountains' rise,
two for one, pleasing my eyes.
The sun rises over the mountain ridge,
at times a red ball, it's fiery light
mitigated by smoke or dust.
And every so often, when not obscured by clouds,
the gibbous moon, ever so bright,
bathes the valley in its silvery light.
At which time I love to entertain friends for dinner
on my deck outside, gazing across the dusky sight.
Occasionally in summertime, towards evening,
I may sit on the deck,
watching the setting sun's shadows creep up
the hillsides across from where I sit,
a kind of meditation leaving behind the day's dross,
mind you, it's no great loss.
Then the summer constellations appear,
Cygnus, little Delphinius, Lyra, and more,
across the vast stellar shore.
Rarely do I see a haboob's sand and dust
blown higher than the mountains' crest.

Lacy virgas fail reaching the ground,
at other times, thunderclouds, pregnant with rain,
crawl threateningly across the ridge,
in a cloudburst to release their load.
At eventide, mist or low clouds drift
into the valley down to the left,
only next morning to reverse in a lift.
Glorious rainbows leave their transient mark,
the real pot of gold, the colors of their arc.
A dusting of early snow
makes a fairyland, a sight to behold,
only to melt in the sun's afternoon glow.
In the sky above ravens cavort,
in summer turkey vultures lazily "float,"
an occasional eagle heads for his redoubt, remote.
In the dark, when coyotes have made a kill,
their howls, wildness exemplified,
a nighttime thrill.
Right close a multitude of bird species feed.
A Cooper's hawk may lurk in a tree,
ready to pounce on a dove, its favorite prey.
In breeding season, early morn',
owls hoot from rooftops in haunting sounds.
'Tis, too, the time, for male doves and quail,
to call for females for a new year's travail.

And a roadrunner's lovelorn hail,
repeated, unrequited, likely bound to fail.
Deer, does and stags, and javelinas tread,
an occasional bobcat, also skunks pass, I concede.
And chipmunks scurry across the rocks
at their reckless, accustomed speed.
To give all this up, sooner or later,
a terrible loss it will be, I fear, indeed.

Beauty of whatever kind, in its supreme development,
invariably excites the sensitive soul to tears.
Edgar Allen Poe

Middlin'

Recently, with my psych-prof friend,
we talked about what IQ scores meant.
My middlin' score I had always bemoaned,
having wished for a higher one,
more brainier domed.
When I subsequently googled the ratings list
I found it means "superior and gifted,"
falling into only six percent.
It drove home the point why mankind is
is in trouble and misery.
And should you consider this hypocrisy,
I can only laugh as to where this leaves me.
At eighty-one I don't give a damn.
Take it or leave it.
Live with my charm.

The magic of fiction lies in deluding reason
that it is fiction.
Róbert Gál

Birthday Gift

At a doctor's office, the other day,
I made an appointment to be seen again.
The new receptionist,
a good-looking sixty year-old,
looked at the computer for my data,
and said: "Oh, your birthday's coming up."
And I, leaning on the counter, responded with:
"Yeah, and it's eighty-one years."
She looked up at me
and said only one word:
"No."
One of the nicest birthdays gifts
I've had.

We ascribe beauty to that which is simple;
which has no superfluous parts;
which exactly answers its end;
which stands related to all things;
which is the mean of many extremes.
Ralph Waldo Emerson

Moving Mass

Have you observed the movement of birds,
of lizards, and other small fry?
How jerkily their body parts move,
up, down, left and right.
Their bodies are small,
little weight need be moved,
but going up the ladder of life,
with size, jerky movement is supplemented
by continuous motion,
with mass, that is weight having increased.
Then, when the size, the bulk of a creature
comes into play,
it makes for elephants' stately walking sway.

To imagine is everything, to know is nothing at all.
Anatole France

Heat Transfer

The oceans having warmed,
there's more evaporation.
The water has to go somewhere,
for the skies can't hold it all,
so there is precipitation.
Commonly called it comes down as rain,
and when there's too much
causes plenty of pain.
For how much longer
will denial reign?

A cynic is one who knows the price of everything
and the value of nothing.
Oscar Wilde

Why Not

Fifty years, almost two generations ago,
looking at the ceiling of my motel room
somewhere in LA,
I noticed the sparkle of glass splinters
in the stucco decor.
I thought "oh, how kitschy,"
but not much later imagined it resembling
an appealing starry sky.
At the time I was fighting a battle
with an entrenched ruling clique
at the German parent company,
mostly engineers intent on selling
what they thought was chic,
what they thought right for the client to buy.
I introduced to them the statement "Why not!"
to accommodate the buyers,
and sell more, by and by,
but heard from them only
the drawn-out word "whhhy."
The "why not" is what makes America
fly so high.

Misfortune seldom intrudes upon the wise man,
his greatest and highest interests are directed by reason
throughout the course of life.
Epicurus

Droning

There are folks who keep droning on
about a subject of interest largely to them.
A book they've read, a movie they've seen,
or whatever it is they are ardent about, keen.
They lose all track in their ongoing spiel,
and bore the heck out of their audience
with their unaware zeal.

What we obtain too cheap we esteem too little;
it is dearness that gives everything its value.
Thomas Paine

Acquisitions

In the past, the means acquired,
I picked up many things,
books, objects of art and handicraft,
attractive, beautiful, to be admired.
Inside my home but outside, too,
interesting rocks from around the world,
mind you, none too big, to carry to.
There's other "stuff"
which piled up through the years
I have no more use for,
no more music to my ears.
Thus I've arrived at this stage of life
when I part from acquisitions
I no longer have need for,
but am glad to surrender
to someone else's delight.

The slope contains many wonders
not found at the summit.
Marty Rubin

Chikungunya

Hardly anyone knows of it,
a mosquito-borne des206ease
quite widespread now.
First diagnosed in southern Tanzania.
In the local Makonde language meaning
"to become contorted, bent forward."
Well, in two thousand-fourteen I safaried there.
Who knows what I might have picked up?
So, when, these days,
I no longer walk tall and straight
I wonder whether it's caused
by chikungunya or age.

Experience increases our wisdom but doesn't reduce our
follies.
Henry Wheeler Shaw

Redeemstress

*I wonder why the Christian God
didn't dispatch His daughter
to redeem humanity's lot?*

Believe those who are seeking the truth.
Doubt those who find it.
Andre Gide

Life

is chaos,
to which we try to bring order!
Here and there we succeed,
then think all is well,
when in fact just beyond may lurk holy hell.
The Greeks called the Universe
"Cosmos," meaning order.
We still believe this,
but only because our lives
are so very much shorter.
We must see galaxies, suns, planets,
black holes, moons, and everything else,
as temporary manifestations,
all living and dying,
just a "bit" longer than humanity's lot.
Death is the only, the final order,
with peace just beyond all life's ephemeral border.

Death twitches my ear. "Live," he says, "I am waiting."
Virgil

And in Ecclesiastes it is written:

"For everything there is a season;
a time to be born, and a time to die;
a time to plant, and a time to reap;
a time to kill, and a time to heal;
a time to build, and a time to tear down;
a time to weep, and a time to laugh;
a time to mourn, and a time to dance;
a time to discard, and a time to collect;
a time to embrace, and a time to spurn;
a time to seek, and a time to lose;
a time to keep, and a time to dispose;
a time to tear, and a time to sew;
a time to be silent, and a time to speak;
a time to love, and a time to hate;
a time for war, and a time for peace."

Death twitches my ear. "Come," he says, "I love you."
Herbert Windolf

About the Author

Born in 1936 in Wiesbaden, Germany, Herbert Windolf is a German citizen. Since the early 1990s, he and his wife, Ute, have resided in Prescott, Arizona. Married in 1961, they have three children.

At age twenty Herbert undertook a motorcycle trip through Libya and Egypt, followed in 1960 by a work assignment in Paris, France, both impacting his subsequent life.

In 1964, he joined his German employer, a machine tool company, as a

Photo by Forrest Jones

technician for transfer to Canada, and in 1970 relocated to Chicago, Illinois, as sales manager. He became managing director, then vice-president of the U.S. affiliate and eventually the importer for the company.

After moving to Prescott, he facilitated various scientific courses at a local adult education center. He holds a bachelor's degree in anthropology.

He has translated and published twenty-two books, seventeen of Karl May's, comprised of forty novels, novellas, and short stories (from German to English), including five hundred poems, and has written a biographical account of his wife's grandparents and parents who were Lutheran missionaries in Sumatra.

Widely traveled, he has written and published numerous travelogues. These, together with his scientific articles, were published in the Quarterly of the Planetary Studies Foundation, where he is Vice-President Emeritus. An astronomer friend has named an asteroid after him.

This fifth book of poems, *Contemplations*, continues Herb's views expounded in *Observations and Reflections, Pondering What Is, Otherwise, and Musings*.

Made in the USA
Columbia, SC
15 November 2017